The Book On

Persuasion

Ethical Influence Without Manipulation

The Book On Series

Alex Mercer

Published by The Book On Publishing, 2025.

First edition. October 19, 2025

Website: https://thebookon.ca

Substack: https://thebookonpublishing.substack.com/

The Book On Persuasion: Ethical Influence Without Manipulation
First edition. October 19, 2025

Copyright © 2025 The Book On Publishing
ISBN: 978-1-997909-40-8

Written by Dr. Alex Mercer

The Book On Series

Table Of Contents

Chapter 1: The Art of Influence: Understanding Persuasion

Every conversation carries within it a hidden architecture of influence. When a child convinces a parent to extend bedtime by fifteen minutes, when a nonprofit director secures funding from a hesitant board member, when a product designer shapes user behavior through interface choice persuasion is at work. Yet most people navigate these moments of influence unconsciously, unaware of the psychological mechanisms operating beneath the surface of human interaction. Understanding persuasion means recognizing that influence is neither mystical nor manipulative by nature; it is simply the fundamental process through which ideas, beliefs, and behaviors move between minds. This chapter explores persuasion as both art and science, examining how it operates in daily life and why mastering its principles transforms not only outcomes but also relationships, leadership effectiveness, and the capacity to create meaningful change.

The word "persuasion" derives from the Latin *persuadere*, meaning "to thoroughly advise" or "to convince sweetly." This etymology reveals something essential: genuine persuasion involves guidance rather than coercion, invitation rather than force. Consider the difference between a salesperson who pressures you into an unwanted purchase and one who helps you discover a solution that genuinely addresses your needs. The first creates resistance and regret; the second generates gratitude and trust. This distinction illuminates why persuasion, when practiced thoughtfully, strengthens human connections rather than exploiting them.
Throughout history, societies have grappled with the power of persuasive communication—from ancient Greek

philosophers debating the role of rhetoric in democracy to modern researchers using brain imaging to understand decision-making processes. Yet the core challenge remains unchanged: how do we influence others' thinking and behavior while respecting their autonomy and serving their interests alongside our own?

The Persuasion Ecosystem: Where Influence Lives

Persuasion exists everywhere that humans interact, creating what might be called a "persuasion ecosystem"a complex network of influence attempts co-occurring across multiple domains. In the professional realm, persuasion manifests in negotiations, where parties seek mutually beneficial outcomes; in presentations, where leaders must inspire teams toward ambitious goals; and in customer interactions, where value must be communicated compellingly. A manager persuading an employee to take on additional responsibilities isn't merely assigning tasks; she's shaping that person's career trajectory and self-concept. The employee's response depends on numerous factors: his perception of the manager's credibility, his own career aspirations, the organizational norms, and his assessment of whether this opportunity represents genuine advancement or exploitation.

Within personal relationships, persuasion operates more subtly but no less powerfully. Parents persuading teenagers to make responsible choices, friends convincing each other to pursue healthier lifestyles, and romantic partners negotiating decisions about shared futures—these moments of influence occur against the backdrop of emotional bonds, shared histories, and implicit understandings about power dynamics. The persuasion ecosystem in intimate relationships differs fundamentally from professional contexts because the stakes extend beyond immediate outcomes to encompass relationship quality, emotional safety, and mutual respect. A partner who "wins" an argument through superior rhetorical skill but damages trust and goodwill has failed at persuasion in its most profound sense.

The digital age has exponentially expanded the persuasion ecosystem, creating new channels and challenges for influence. Social media platforms function as persuasion amplifiers, where messages can reach millions instantly, but attention spans are measured in seconds. A climate scientist trying to persuade the public about the urgency of the environment now competes with entertainment content, misinformation campaigns, and algorithm-driven echo chambers that reinforce existing beliefs. Digital persuasion operates under different rules: visual elements often matter more than logical arguments, emotional resonance determines sharing behavior, and source credibility can be manufactured through followers and engagement metrics. Understanding modern persuasion requires recognizing how technological platforms reshape the fundamental dynamics of influence, creating both unprecedented opportunities and novel obstacles for those seeking to change minds and behaviors.

The persuasion ecosystem also encompasses diverse contexts that shape how influence operates. What succeeds in one setting may fail in another, and the global nature of modern commerce, activism, and communication means that contextual awareness has become inseparable from persuasive competence. Professional environments differ from casual social settings in formality, power dynamics, and expected communication norms. Educational contexts prioritize intellectual development and long-term learning over immediate compliance. Political persuasion operates within frameworks of ideology, group identity, and institutional structures that constrain individual choice. Healthcare settings involve persuasion around life-altering decisions made under stress and uncertainty. Each domain presents unique challenges and opportunities for influence. Persuasion also varies significantly across cultures, with different societies holding distinct views about what constitutes credibility, appropriate emotional expression, and effective argumentation. Chapter 10 explores these cultural dimensions comprehensively, examining how persuasive strategies must adapt across cultural contexts and providing frameworks for effective cross-cultural influence.

Foundational Dimensions of Persuasive Communication

Effective persuasion operates simultaneously across distinct but interconnected dimensions identified by ancient rhetoricians as *logos* (logical appeal), *pathos* (emotional appeal), and *ethos* (credibility based on character). These concepts, articulated over two millennia ago, provide an enduring framework for understanding influence across diverse contexts.

Logos addresses the rational mind through evidence, logical structure, and coherent reasoning. When a financial advisor recommends investment diversification, she relies on market data, historical patterns, and risk-reward calculations. The logical dimension provides intellectual scaffolding that enables people to justify their decisions to themselves and others, thereby creating coherence between recommendations and reasoning. Strong logical appeals demonstrate that conclusions rest on solid foundations rather than arbitrary preference or hidden agenda.

Pathos engages in the emotional dimension of human experience. Consider two retirement savings messages: "Contributing 10% of your salary yields approximately $847,000 by age 65, assuming 7% annual returns" versus "Imagine the freedom of choosing how you spend retirement days—traveling to places you've dreamed of visiting, pursuing hobbies you never had time for, spending unhurried afternoons with grandchildren." Both support identical recommendations but engage different psychological systems. Human decision-making integrates both cognitive and emotional processes—a reality that the next chapter explores in depth, revealing how minds process information and arrive at conclusions. Chapter 4 then builds on this foundation by examining emotional psychology specifically and exploring strategies for creating authentic emotional connection in persuasive communication.

Ethos encompasses the persuader's credibility, trustworthiness, and perceived alignment with audience interests. Research consistently demonstrates that identical messages produce dramatically different results depending on source credibility. A medical recommendation carries more weight from a physician than from a celebrity, even if the words are identical. Credibility is a critical component of persuasive success, and Chapter 5 is dedicated entirely to exploring how it operates—examining its various forms, how it's built across different contexts, and how persuaders can leverage and protect this essential asset.

These dimensions work in concert to create a persuasive impact. Messages strong in logic but devoid of emotional resonance may be intellectually acknowledged yet fail to motivate action. Purely emotional appeals without a logical foundation often produce short-lived enthusiasm that dissipates under scrutiny. And regardless of message quality, influence fails if audiences question the persuader's credibility or suspect ulterior motives. Effective persuaders assess which dimension requires emphasis in particular situations while maintaining sufficient strength across all three. A technical presentation to engineers might emphasize logical rigor, while a fundraising appeal prioritizes emotional connection, yet both require credibility and cannot entirely neglect other dimensions.

The Nature of Receptivity and Resistance

Understanding persuasion requires acknowledging a fundamental reality: people do not passively absorb persuasive messages. Instead, audiences actively evaluate, question, and often resist attempts to influence them, even when accepting them would serve their interests. This dynamic interaction between persuader and audience shapes every influence attempt, and recognizing when people are most receptive to new ideas proves as crucial as crafting compelling messages.

Receptivity to persuasion increases under specific conditions that skilled persuaders learn to recognize and cultivate. Cognitive openness peaks during transitional life phases—such as starting college, changing careers, experiencing relationship changes, or relocating to new communities—when existing mental models are already under pressure and revision becomes necessary. People experiencing uncertainty actively seek information and guidance, creating opportunities for influence. Additionally, positive emotional states increase receptivity; individuals who feel happy, curious, or inspired process information more openly and generate fewer counterarguments than those experiencing negative emotions like anger or fear.

When audiences do resist persuasive messages, that resistance provides valuable information rather than representing mere obstruction. Skepticism signals concerns that must be addressed before substantive persuasion can proceed. The manager whose team resists a new initiative investigates underlying fears or concerns rather than simply repeating arguments more forcefully. Resistance takes many forms—from outright rejection to subtle avoidance, from intellectual disagreement to emotional defensiveness—and understanding why people resist influence attempts proves essential for effective persuasion. Chapter 12 provides comprehensive frameworks for understanding resistance mechanisms, exploring psychological reactance and other defensive responses in depth, and offers specific techniques for transforming resistance from obstacle into opportunity for deeper engagement and more sustainable influence.

Persuasion as Co-Creation Rather Than Conquest

Traditional models often frame persuasion as something one person does to another—the persuader acting upon a passive target, overwhelming resistance through superior technique. This conquest metaphor fundamentally misrepresents how genuine influence operates. Effective persuasion functions less like conquest and more like co-creation, a collaborative process in which both parties actively participate in meaning-making and decision-making. The persuader provides information, frameworks, and perspectives; the audience integrates these elements with existing knowledge, experiences, and values, generating conclusions that feel self-authored rather than imposed. This distinction proves critical because people embrace beliefs, they've reasoned toward themselves far more deeply than conclusions they've merely accepted from external sources.

Consider a financial planner working with clients approaching retirement. The ineffective approach involves prescribing a predetermined strategy, overwhelming clients with expertise, and expecting compliance based on superior knowledge. The practical approach treats planning as collaborative exploration: asking questions that help clients articulate their values and priorities, presenting options with transparent trade-offs, encouraging clients to imagine different scenarios and their emotional responses, and ultimately guiding clients toward decisions they understand and endorse. The second approach takes longer and requires more skill but generates dramatically superior outcomes because clients feel ownership of the resulting strategy. When market downturns occur, clients who meaningfully participated in decision-making maintain confidence in their approach; those who merely followed expert directives experience doubt and may abandon strategies at precisely the wrong moment.

This co-creative model has profound implications for persuasive communication strategies. Rather than constructing monologues designed to overwhelm objections, effective persuaders design dialogues that invite participation. They ask questions more than make statements, listen actively to understand the audience's perspective, and wait to speak rather than merely talk. They acknowledge valid concerns and incorporate them into their messaging rather than dismissing resistance. They provide frameworks for thinking rather than conclusions to accept, empowering audiences to apply principles to their unique circumstances. A manager persuading a team to adopt new software doesn't just list features and mandate adoption; she facilitates discussions about current workflow pain points, invites team members to evaluate how proposed solutions address their specific challenges, and incorporates feedback into implementation planning. The resulting adoption occurs through authentic buy-in rather than grudging compliance.

The co-creative approach also addresses practical concerns about sustainable influence. When influence operates as collaborative meaning-making rather than manipulation, it respects autonomy while exercising influence. The audience member retains agency, making genuine choices based on enhanced understanding rather than being tricked or coerced. People increasingly recognize and resist manipulative persuasion attempts, while authentic, collaborative influence builds trust and long-term relationships that enable sustained influence across multiple interactions. The sales professional, community organizer, or thought leader who has succeeded over decades does so not through clever manipulation but by consistently helping people make decisions that genuinely serve their interests.

The collaborative nature of persuasion also means that effective influencers must be prepared to be influenced by themselves. When you approach persuasion as dialogue rather than monologue, you create space for learning from your audience. Their objections may reveal flaws in your reasoning, their perspectives may illuminate considerations you hadn't contemplated, and their resistance may signal that your proposal genuinely doesn't serve their interests as well as you believed. The persuader who remains rigidly committed to predetermined conclusions regardless of what emerges in conversation has abandoned genuine persuasion for something closer to propaganda or coercion. Authentic influence requires intellectual humility, the willingness to revise your own thinking when evidence warrants, even as you work to shape others' perspectives. This mutual openness to influence doesn't weaken persuasive effectiveness; paradoxically, it strengthens it by building credibility and demonstrating that you value truth and mutual benefit over winning arguments.

The Temporal Dimension: Immediate Impact Versus Lasting Change

Persuasion unfolds across time, and understanding this temporal dimension reveals why some influence attempts produce immediate compliance but fail to generate lasting change. Psychological research distinguishes between different types of attitude change: compliance (behavioral change without belief change), identification (adoption of behaviors or beliefs to maintain relationships), and internalization (genuine integration of new perspectives into one's belief system). A teenager who cleans his room only when his parents threaten consequences demonstrates compliance; his behavior changes, but his underlying attitudes remain unchanged, and compliance disappears when surveillance ends. An employee who adopts a manager's perspective to maintain a positive relationship demonstrates identification; the influence depends on the relationship's continuation. Internalization represents the deepest form of persuasion, in which new beliefs are authentically incorporated into one's worldview and persist independent of external rewards, punishments, or relationship dynamics.

Effective long-term persuasion prioritizes internalization by helping people develop a genuine understanding of why specific beliefs or behaviors serve their interests and values. This requires patience and sophistication beyond approaches that focus on immediate compliance. Parents teaching children financial responsibility could demand allowance savings through rules and consequences (compliance), or they could involve children in family budget discussions, help them set personal goals that require saving, let them experience the natural consequences of spending decisions, and celebrate their progress (internalization). The second approach takes far longer and requires more parental skills and emotional regulation but produces adults who genuinely value financial responsibility rather than merely performing required behaviors when monitored.

The temporal dimension also encompasses the spacing and sequencing of persuasive messages. Single exposure to information rarely changes minds on significant issues; instead, influence typically requires multiple exposures across time, allowing audiences to encounter ideas repeatedly from different angles and in various contexts. Marketing professionals understand this principle intimately: effective campaigns expose audiences to core messages across diverse channels and formats, fostering familiarity and enabling gradual attitude evolution. Social movements changing cultural attitudes about issues like smoking, drunk driving, or environmental responsibility succeed through sustained communication efforts spanning years or decades, not through a single powerful message. The persuader's timeline must match the magnitude of change sought—minor behavioral adjustments may occur rapidly, but fundamental belief revision requires patience and persistent, varied engagement.

Additionally, persuasion effectiveness depends significantly on timing relative to decision points and implementation opportunities. Information most powerfully influences behavior when delivered close to the moment when action becomes possible. Public health campaigns promoting flu vaccination are most effective in early fall, when vaccines become available, rather than mid-summer, when the message seems abstract and irrelevant. Similarly, persuading employees to adopt new technologies works best when the tools become available and training is scheduled, not months earlier when enthusiasm wanes before implementation begins. Strategic persuaders consider not just message content but optimal delivery timing, recognizing that identical messages produce vastly different results depending on when audiences encounter them relative to their decision-making processes and action opportunities.

The relationship between immediate and long-term persuasion also involves understanding how small commitments can build toward larger ones. Social psychologists have documented the "foot-in-the-door" phenomenon, in which people who agree to small initial requests are more likely to agree to larger subsequent requests. This occurs partly because the initial commitment shapes self-perception—having agreed to a small action consistent with specific values or identities, people see themselves as the type of person who supports such causes, making larger commitments psychologically consistent. Environmental organizations successfully use this principle: first asking households to display window stickers supporting conservation, then later requesting more substantial obligations, such as installing solar panels or changing consumption habits. The initial small commitment costs little but shifts identity in ways that facilitate later influence. Understanding these temporal dynamics allows persuaders to design influence campaigns that build momentum progressively rather than demanding immediate, dramatic change that triggers resistance.

Developing Persuasive Mastery: The Path Forward

Mastering persuasion requires both intellectual understanding and practical skill development through deliberate practice and reflective experience. Unlike purely cognitive skills that can be learned through study alone, persuasion demands real-world application where theory meets the complexity of human psychology, unpredictable reactions, and situational nuances. The journey toward persuasive mastery begins with systematic observation— paying constant attention to influence attempts around you, analyzing what works and what fails, and identifying the patterns underlying successful persuasion across diverse contexts. Watch skilled negotiators, effective teachers, compelling speakers, and successful salespeople, noting not just what they say but how they create rapport, structure arguments, handle objections, and adapt to audience responses in real-time.

Self-awareness represents another critical dimension of persuasive development. Effective persuaders understand their own biases, communication tendencies, and emotional triggers that might interfere with strategic influence. Someone who becomes defensive when questioned will struggle with persuasion, as handling objections gracefully is essential to influencing success. Similarly, persuaders must recognize their credibility assets and liabilities with different audiences. Experience valued in one context may prove irrelevant or even counterproductive in another. A technology executive carries enormous credibility when discussing innovation with engineers but may lack credibility when addressing work-life balance concerns with employees, at least initially. Self-aware persuaders leverage their credibility strengths while expanding their influence capacity in domains where they start from weaker positions.

Developing persuasive capability also requires cultivating specific communication competencies that enable effective influence. Active listening, truly hearing and understanding others' perspectives rather than merely waiting for your turn to speak—forms the foundation of collaborative persuasion.

Skilled persuaders ask probing questions that help audiences articulate their own thinking, revealing both opportunities for influence and potential obstacles requiring address. They demonstrate empathy, showing genuine understanding of others' concerns and validating emotions even while working to shift perspectives. They exhibit flexibility, adapting their approach based on audience responses rather than rigidly following predetermined scripts. They manage their own emotional states, maintaining composure and positivity even when facing resistance or hostility. These competencies develop through conscious practice and reflection, gradually becoming more natural and automatic with experience.

The intellectual dimension of persuasive mastery involves building knowledge across multiple domains relevant to influence. Understanding introductory psychology provides insight into how people think, feel, and make decisions—knowledge that the following chapter will begin developing systematically. Studying communication theory illuminates how messages are constructed, transmitted, and interpreted. Learning about specific contexts where you seek influence—whether business, politics, education, or personal relationships—provides domain expertise that enhances credibility and enables more relevant, compelling arguments. Reading widely exposes you to diverse perspectives and rhetorical approaches, expanding your repertoire of persuasive strategies. The most effective persuaders are often intellectually curious generalists who can draw connections across domains, finding unexpected analogies and frameworks that make complex ideas accessible and compelling.

The chapters ahead will systematically build your understanding of persuasion's psychological foundations and practical applications. The next chapter explores the psychology of decision-making, revealing how the human mind actually processes information and arrives at conclusions essential for anyone seeking to influence those processes effectively. You'll discover specific techniques that enhance persuasive effectiveness across contexts, learn how to craft messages for maximum impact, understand the unique dynamics of group influence, and develop frameworks to navigate the complex responsibilities that accompany persuasive power. Each chapter builds on the foundation established here, progressively developing both your conceptual understanding and practical capability.

Understanding persuasion's foundational nature, recognizing it as collaborative meaning-making operating across multiple dimensions, acknowledging the dynamic interplay between receptivity and resistance, and appreciating the temporal aspects of genuine change— provides the essential framework for all subsequent learning. Persuasion represents one of humanity's most consequential capabilities, shaping individual lives, organizational outcomes, and cultural evolution. Approaching this power with both sophistication and responsibility positions you not merely achieve your goals but create positive influence that improves decision-making, strengthens relationships, and generates outcomes that benefit everyone involved. The art of influence, practiced with skill and integrity, becomes not manipulation but genuine service, helping others see possibilities, understand their interests more clearly, and make choices that enhance their lives while advancing shared purposes. This is the promise and potential of mastering persuasion, and the journey toward that mastery begins with the foundational understanding established in this chapter and continues through the systematic exploration of persuasive principles and practices in the pages ahead.

Chapter 2: The Psychology of Decision-Making

When someone decides to purchase a particular brand of coffee, accepts a job offer, or trust a stranger's recommendation, they typically believe they've made a conscious, deliberate choice based on careful consideration of available information. Yet beneath this surface experience of rational deliberation lies a far more complex reality. Our decisions emerge from the interaction of multiple neural systems—some ancient and automatic, others recently evolved and deliberative—each processing different types of information and operating according to distinct rules. This chapter explores the architecture of human decision-making, revealing how our minds work when confronted with choices, and what these mechanisms mean for anyone seeking to influence decisions effectively.

Understanding these systems —their strengths and limitations, and how they interact — transforms persuasion from guesswork into a more systematic practice grounded in cognitive science. As we established in the previous chapter, persuasion operates through recognizable patterns and principles. Now we examine the psychological machinery that makes these patterns effective—the cognitive processes that determine how people evaluate information, form judgments, and ultimately make choices. This foundation proves essential for everything that follows, from crafting compelling messages to navigating resistance and building lasting influence.

Cognitive Biases as Decision-Making Signatures

Our cognitive architecture processes information through patterns that produce systematic errors—what researchers call cognitive biases. These aren't random mistakes or signs of stupidity; they're predictable signatures of how our mental systems handle information, reflecting evolutionary adaptations that generally served our ancestors well but can mislead us in modern contexts. The anchoring effect demonstrates this vividly. When judges with decades of experience were asked to sentence convicted criminals, researchers found their decisions were systematically influenced by random numbers presented immediately beforehand. In one study, judges rolled dice (secretly loaded to show either three or nine) before deliberating sentencing. Those who rolled nine imposed sentences that were 50% longer than those who rolled three, despite all judges seeing identical case files and explicitly knowing the dice roll was random and irrelevant. The mere presence of a number, even one obviously unrelated to the decision, created an "anchor" that subsequent judgment adjusted from, demonstrating how associative processing shapes even supposedly rational deliberation.

The endowment effect reveals another systematic pattern in decision-making that persuaders must understand. People assign significantly higher value to things they own than to identical items they might acquire, a phenomenon economist Richard Thaler demonstrated through experiments with coffee mugs. When researchers randomly distributed mugs to half of a group's participants and then allowed trading, classical economic theory predicted that approximately half the mugs would change hands as people discovered their valid preferences. Instead, remarkably few trades occurred. People who were randomly given mugs demanded prices roughly twice as high as non-owners were willing to pay for identical mugs. This wasn't about the mugs' objective value but about psychological ownership. Once something becomes "ours," we perceive it differently automatic processing assigns a premium to possessions that it doesn't to hypothetical acquisitions. Real estate agents exploit this by encouraging potential buyers to imagine themselves living in properties, mentally taking ownership before actual purchase. Free trial periods leverage the endowment effect by creating a sense of temporary ownership, making surrender (cancellation) feel like a loss rather than the avoidance of a new expense.

How information is presented—its frame—dramatically changes decisions even when objective outcomes remain identical. Medical patients who have shown that a surgical procedure has a "90% survival rate" respond more favorably than those said it has a "10% mortality rate," despite the statements being mathematically identical. The positive frame emphasizes what will be gained or preserved, while the negative frame highlights potential loss. This pattern reflects loss aversion—potential losses weigh roughly twice as heavily as equivalent gains in our psychological calculus. This asymmetry shapes everything from purchasing behavior to international diplomacy, where political leaders accept greater risks to avoid perceived losses than to achieve equivalent gains. The linguistic dimensions of framing and its practical applications in message construction will be explored in depth in the next chapter, but understanding its psychological foundation reveals a core principle: our minds respond to presentation context, not just content.

Confirmation bias, perhaps the most pervasive cognitive distortion, describes our tendency to seek, interpret, and remember information that confirms existing beliefs while discounting contradictory evidence. Once we form an initial hypothesis or impression, our minds operate as though we were proving rather than testing it, selectively attending to supporting information. In one experiment, researchers asked participants with strong opinions about capital punishment to evaluate two studies—one showing death penalties deter crime, another showing they don't. Rather than moderating views considering mixed evidence, participants on both sides found the study supporting their pre-existing position methodologically sound and the contradicting study fatally flawed. Identical evidence strengthened opposing views because different standards of evaluation were automatically applied to congenial versus uncongenial findings. This explains why presenting contradictory facts often fails to change minds and can strengthen existing beliefs—a phenomenon researchers call the "backfire effect." Understanding confirmation bias reveals why persuasion requires approaches far more sophisticated than simply marshaling superior evidence, particularly when addressing established viewpoints.

The Paradox of Choice and Decision Fatigue

While conventional wisdom suggests more options that always benefit decision-makers, psychological research reveals a more complex relationship between choice abundance and decision quality. Psychologist Barry Schwartz's experiments demonstrated what he termed the "paradox of choice". Beyond a certain point, additional options diminish rather than enhance decision satisfaction and can even paralyze decision-making entirely. In now-classic studies, researchers set up tasting booths at a grocery store, offering either six or twenty-four varieties of gourmet jam. The extensive selection attracted more initial interest, but the limited selection produced dramatically better results: 30% of people who stopped at the six-jam display made purchases, compared to only 3% of those exposed to twenty-four options. The abundance that seemed advantageous overwhelmed analytical capacity, leading people to defer decisions entirely rather than work through extensive comparisons. When purchases did occur, buyers who chose from limited options reported greater satisfaction with their selections than those who chose from extensive arrays, suggesting that option abundance undermines not just decision-making but also post-decision satisfaction.

This phenomenon relates to decision fatigue—the deterioration in decision-making quality after extended periods of decision-making. Our capacity for careful deliberation is a limited resource that depletes with use. Research examining consumer behavior finds that people shopping later in extended browsing sessions make increasingly impulsive or poor-quality decisions. Students selecting courses near registration deadlines choose less optimally than those registering early. Negotiators making concessions late in protracted discussions often agree to terms they would have rejected earlier when mental resources were fresh. The implications of decision fatigue for the timing of persuasive appeals will be explored in detail in Chapter 11, where we examine Chronopsychology and the temporal dimensions of influence. Still, the basic mechanism deserves attention here: as effortful thinking becomes depleted, judgments increasingly reflect automatic, heuristic-based responses rather than careful analysis.

Understanding these patterns transforms how effective persuaders present choices. Rather than overwhelming audiences with extensive options, skilled communicators carefully curate limited alternatives that facilitate rather than paralyzing decision-making. When Amazon simplified its checkout process and reduced the number of decisions required, conversion rates increased significantly, despite seemingly giving customers less control. The company recognized that each decision point depleted limited mental resources and created opportunities for abandonment.

Political consultants know that complex ballot measures with numerous provisions tend to fail, regardless of their individual merit, because voters, confronted with long lists of issues, increasingly rely on status quo bias when analytical thinking becomes overwhelmed. Public health advocates promoting behavior change avoid presenting elaborate multi-step programs that require sustained deliberative engagement; instead, they break changes into simple, sequential decisions that don't tax mental resources.

Heuristics: The Mind's Shortcuts and Their Persuasive Implications

Beyond specific biases, our minds employ general heuristic rules of thumb for making judgments efficiently when complete analysis would be impractical or impossible. The availability heuristic influences decisions whenever we estimate frequency, probability, or causation based on how easily examples come to mind rather than actual data. When asked to assess the likelihood of dying in a terrorist attack versus dying in a car accident, most people dramatically overestimate terrorism risk and underestimate automotive risk, despite car accidents killing vastly more people annually. This occurs because judgment relies on availability—how easily examples come to mind—rather than actual statistical frequency. Terrorist attacks receive extensive media coverage and create vivid, memorable images that are readily recalled. Car accidents, being commonplace, generate less dramatic mental imagery despite being statistically more dangerous. Married couples consistently overestimate their own contributions to household tasks relative to their partner's contributions, not from dishonesty but because their own actions are more cognitively available—more readily recalled—than behaviors they didn't personally perform.

For persuaders, the availability heuristic explains why vivid, concrete examples often influence decisions more than comprehensive statistics. Charitable organizations know that featuring one named child needing help generates more donations than citing statistics about millions in need, because a specific face and story create memorable, emotionally resonant cognitive availability that aggregate numbers cannot. This isn't manipulation but rather working with how memory and judgment function. However, the exact mechanism enables fearmongering and misinformation. Repeatedly exposing people to dramatic but statistically rare danger shark attacks, plane crashes, stranger kidnappings—makes these risks cognitively available, leading to inflated probability estimates and fear responses disproportionate to actual threat. Repetition itself creates availability; a claim repeated frequently becomes easier to recall and, therefore, judged more credible, regardless of its evidentiary support. This "illusory truth effect" means persuaders can shape perceived reality simply by controlling which information becomes cognitively available through repetition and emphasis.

Representative heuristics lead people to judge probability based on how well something matches mental prototypes rather than actual statistical likelihood. When told that "John is quiet, organized, and enjoys reading," most people guess he's more likely to be a librarian than a farmer, despite farmers vastly outnumbering librarians. John matches our mental prototype of librarians better than farmers, so representativeness trumps base-rate probability. This heuristic can lead to stereotyping and serious judgment errors, but it also reveals how people process information about categories and individuals. Personal branding exploits representativeness by cultivating images that match prototypes of credibility and expertise—tech entrepreneurs wearing black turtlenecks, financial advisors in conservative suits, creative professionals in casual attire—all signaling category membership through representative characteristics. Political candidates craft personas that match voter prototypes of leadership, competence, or authenticity, knowing that representativeness influences perceived suitability more than detailed policy analysis does for most voters.

Social proof represents another powerful heuristic that shapes decisions across countless contexts. When uncertain about how to behave or what to choose, people look to others' actions for guidance. Restaurant customers gravitate toward busy establishments, assuming crowds indicate quality. Online shoppers rely heavily on product reviews and ratings. Individuals confronted with emergencies often fail to act when surrounded by passive bystanders, each person taking cues from others' inaction. The mechanisms underlying social proof and its applications in persuasion are sufficiently complex and essential that Chapter 6 dedicates comprehensive attention to social influence, conformity dynamics, and group behavior. For now, recognizing social proof as one heuristic among many establishes its place in the broader landscape of decision-making shortcuts that persuaders must understand.

The effect heuristic describes how emotional responses serve as information shortcuts—we judge things we feel good about as having higher benefits and lower risks. In contrast, things generating negative feelings seem riskier and less beneficial. Nuclear engineers and activists evaluate nuclear power completely differently, not because they analyze different data but because their emotional responses shape risk perception. Engineers' positive effect leads them to see high benefits and low risks; activists' negative affect leads them to see the opposite. Neither group is simply rational or irrational; both are human decision-makers whose emotions function as heuristic guides to judgment. Smart persuaders recognize that influencing the effect associated with options often changes decisions more effectively than presenting logical arguments. Pharmaceutical naming illustrates this principle: drugs with easier-to-pronounce names are judged safer than those with complex names, because processing fluency creates positive affect that transfers to safety judgments. Design choices, color schemes, ambient music, and countless environmental factors shape affective responses that then guide ostensibly rational decisions through the affect heuristic's operation.

The Interplay of Emotion and Reason in Decision-Making

The relationship between emotional and cognitive systems in decision-making deserves particular attention, as it fundamentally shapes how persuasion operates. Traditional models portrayed emotion and reason as opposing forces, with rational deliberation representing the ideal and emotional influence constituting a regrettable contamination of pure logic. Contemporary neuroscience and psychology reveal a far different picture: emotion and cognition function as integrated systems, with emotional processing providing essential information that enables rather than undermines effective decision-making.

Neuroscientist Antonio Damasio's research with patients suffering damage to brain regions processing emotion demonstrated this integration dramatically. These patients retained standard intellectual capabilities—they could analyze options logically, calculate probabilities, and articulate the pros and cons of different choices. Yet they struggled profoundly with even simple real-world decisions, spending hours deliberating over trivial choices like where to eat lunch. Without emotional signals indicating whether options were desirable or aversive, they lacked a mechanism for valuing alternatives or terminating analysis. Their experience revealed that emotion doesn't corrupt rational thought; it provides the evaluative framework that makes practical reasoning possible.

Emotions serve multiple functions in decision-making. They focus attention on information relevant to current concerns and goals. Fear directs cognitive resources toward potential threats; excitement highlights opportunities; guilt signals violations of personal standards. These emotional responses operate rapidly, often before conscious awareness, preparing behavioral responses and shaping which information receives analytical attention. The effect heuristic, discussed earlier, represents one manifestation of this broader pattern—emotional responses provide quick evaluative judgments that guide decisions when thorough analysis would be impractical.

Emotions also encode learning from past experiences. When we encounter situations similar to those that previously produced positive or negative outcomes, emotional responses automatically activate, providing rapid guidance based on accumulated experience. Someone who suffered food poisoning from seafood experiences automatic aversion when considering seafood options, even if they can't consciously recall the specific incident. An investor who profited from a particular strategy feels a positive effect toward similar opportunities. These emotional memories operate independently of conscious recollection, influencing decisions through affective responses that may seem intuitive or instinctive.

For persuaders, understanding emotion's role in decision-making transforms practice in crucial ways. Rather than viewing emotional appeals as somehow less legitimate than logical arguments, effective communicators recognize that engaging both emotional and cognitive systems produces more complete and compelling persuasion. A public health campaign promoting vaccination succeeds not just by presenting statistical evidence of efficacy (engaging analytical processing) but also by evoking protective feelings toward loved ones and relief at preventing disease (engaging emotional processing). A financial advisor helps clients make sound investment decisions not only through numerical analysis but also by addressing the anxiety, hope, and fear that inevitably accompany financial choices.

The ethical implications deserve emphasis. Engaging emotions in persuasion isn't inherently manipulative; it's recognizing how human decision-making works. However, emotional appeals can be used ethically or unethically depending on whether they serve the audience's genuine interests. Evoking fear about legitimate risks to motivate protective behavior differs fundamentally from manufacturing baseless anxiety to sell unnecessary products. Inspiring hope about achievable goals differs from making false promises. The distinction lies not in whether emotions are engaged but in whether that engagement serves truth and the audience's welfare. Chapter 4 will explore emotional appeals in depth, examining how to engage feelings ethically and effectively. For now, establishing that emotion and reason function as integrated rather than opposing systems provides an essential foundation for understanding persuasion's psychological basis.

Mental Accounting and the Psychology of Value

The way people mentally categorize and evaluate financial decisions reveals systematic patterns that deviate from economic rationality but follow psychological logic. Mental accounting, a framework developed by Richard Thaler, describes how people create separate cognitive accounts for different types of money and spending, treating economically identical amounts differently based on arbitrary categories. Someone might refuse to spend forty dollars on expedited shipping because it feels wasteful, then impulsively purchase a forty-dollar restaurant meal without deliberation, despite both being identical expenditures. The shipping fee comes from a "necessary expense" mental account, where spending generates guilt, while the meal comes from an "entertainment" account, where spending feels justified. These mental accounts aren't economically logical—money is fungible, and forty dollars has identical value regardless of spending category—but they powerfully shape actual behavior.

The implications for persuasion are substantial. Credit card companies understand that mental accounting makes credit card spending psychologically easier than cash spending because credit purchases draw from a different (more abstract, less painful) mental account than cash payments. The physical act of surrendering paper currency triggers loss aversion and budget awareness that swiping plastic circumvents. Restaurants notice higher tips and more dessert orders when customers pay by card rather than cash, even though the actual cost is the same. Effective price framing exploits mental accounting by shifting expenses between psychological categories: describing a gym membership as "less than a dollar per day" moves the expense from a large lump-sum account to a negligible daily account, making the same price feel more acceptable. Bundling products together obscures individual item costs, while unbundling makes premium components seem like special indulgences rather than price increases—all operating through mental accounting's psychological rather than economic logic.

Sunk cost fallacy represents another deviation from economic rationality that mental accounting explains. People continue investing in failing projects because they've already invested resources, even when economic analysis indicates that past investments should be ignored when evaluating future options. A couple might stay for a terrible movie because they "already paid for tickets," even though the money is gone either way, and leaving would maximize their actual well-being. Businesses continue funding doomed products because of prior investments rather than current prospects. This behavior makes no economic sense—rational analysis evaluates only future costs and benefits, treating past investments as irrelevant sunk costs—but it makes psychological sense within the framework of mental accounting. The psychological account associated with a project includes already-invested resources, and abandoning the project forces acknowledging those investments as losses. Continuing feels like protecting the investment, even though additional resources are wasted on situations that are unredeemable.

Persuaders can either exploit sunk cost thinking or help people overcome it, depending on their goals and ethics. Subscription services leverage sunk costs by making cancellation feel like a waste of prior payments, encouraging continued membership even when the service no longer provides value. Fitness clubs' profit from members who maintain memberships long after stopping attendance because canceling means acknowledging the sunk cost of unused past payments. Conversely, helping people make better decisions often requires countering sunk cost thinking by refocusing attention on future consequences rather than past investments. A financial advisor might help a client exit a poor investment by explicitly reframing the decision: "The question isn't whether you've lost money already—that's gone regardless—but whether this investment will gain or lose money going forward compared to alternatives." This reframing activates analytical capabilities to override the sunk cost instinct, though doing so requires conscious effort that people typically resist.

Resistance and Reactance: The Psychology of Pushback

Understanding decision-making requires examining not only how people accept influence but also why and how they resist it. Psychological reactance, a concept developed by Jack Brehm, describes the motivational state that emerges when people perceive threats to their freedom of choice. When someone feels pressured, commanded, or manipulated, they experience reactance—an uncomfortable tension that motivates them to reassert their autonomy, often by doing the opposite of what's suggested. Teenagers who are told they cannot date someone usually become more attracted to that person. Consumers exposed to high-pressure sales tactics frequently reject offers they might otherwise have accepted. Citizens facing government mandates sometimes resist compliance specifically because the requirement threatens their sense of freedom, even when they might have voluntarily chosen the same behavior.

Reactance explains why overtly persuasive messages often backfire. When persuasive intent becomes too apparent, audiences perceive manipulation attempts that trigger defensive responses. The very act of recognizing that "someone is trying to persuade me" activates skepticism and counterarguing, undermining influence. This creates a paradox for persuaders: the more transparently persuasive a message becomes, the more likely it is to trigger reactance that defeats its purpose. Skilled communicators navigate this challenge through approaches that preserve audience autonomy. Rather than demanding compliance, they present options and allow choice. Instead of claiming superiority, they acknowledge alternatives while highlighting particular benefits. They frame influence attempts as information sharing rather than pressure, reducing perceived threats to freedom that trigger reactance.

Confirmation bias, discussed earlier as a cognitive pattern, also functions as a resistance mechanism. When confronted with information that contradicts established beliefs, people don't simply update their views based on the evidence. Instead, they engage in motivated reasoning—selectively scrutinizing incongruent information while accepting congenial information uncritically. This asymmetric processing protects existing beliefs from challenge, creating resistance that pure evidence cannot overcome. Someone who believes vaccines cause autism will find methodological flaws in studies showing vaccine safety while accepting far weaker evidence supporting their position. A political partisan will dismiss credible reporting about their preferred candidate's misconduct while readily believing similar accusations about opponents. This isn't stupidity or dishonesty; it's how human cognition protects coherent worldviews from constant disruption.

The implications for persuasion are profound. Directly confronting established beliefs with contradictory evidence typically strengthens rather than weakens those beliefs through the backfire effect. When someone's identity or worldview aligns with a belief, challenging that belief feels like an attack on their sense of self, triggering defensive responses that further entrench positions. Effective persuaders recognize these resistance mechanisms and develop strategies that work with rather than against them. Later chapters will explore comprehensive approaches for navigating resistance, building on the psychological foundations established here. For now, understanding that resistance emerges from psychological reactance and motivated reasoning reveals why persuasion requires far more sophistication than simply presenting superior arguments.

Integrating Decision-Making Psychology into Persuasive Practice

The journey through decision-making psychology reveals a consistent theme: human judgment operates through systematic patterns that reflect the design of our cognitive architecture. Our minds employ heuristics that enable rapid judgment but create predictable biases. We construct mental accounts that organize financial decisions according to psychological rather than economic logic. We resist perceived threats to autonomy through reactance and protect established beliefs through motivated reasoning. We experience decision fatigue, which depletes mental resources and distorts our judgment. Emotions and cognition function as integrated systems, with feelings providing essential evaluative information that enables practical choice. Understanding these mechanisms doesn't yield simple manipulation formulas; instead, it reveals the cognitive landscape in which persuasion operates.

Chapter 3: Crafting Compelling Messages: The Power of Language

Words create worlds. A physician describing a medical procedure as having a "ninety percent success rate" elicits entirely different patient responses than saying it has a "ten percent failure rate," despite the two statements being mathematically identical. A manager who tells her team they're "facing challenges" initiates different psychological responses than one who declares they're "confronting obstacles" or "encountering opportunities for innovation." The specific language we select when crafting persuasive messages doesn't merely convey information, it actively shapes how audiences perceive reality, process arguments, and ultimately make decisions. Understanding the nuanced power of linguistic choices transforms persuasion from crude messaging into sophisticated communication architecture.

The science of linguistic persuasion reveals that seemingly minor variations in word selection, sentence structure, and rhetorical devices produce measurable differences in audience receptivity and behavioral outcomes. Neurolinguistic research demonstrates that different words activate distinct neural networks even when referring to the same underlying concept. When experimental subjects read the word "perfume," their olfactory cortex shows increased activity; when they encounter "stench" describing the same scent in a different context, disgust-related neural regions activate. This neurological reality means persuaders don't simply tell an objective world; they linguistically construct the experiential framework through which audiences encounter ideas. The messages we craft literally shape the mental landscapes audiences inhabit as they consider our proposals.

Beyond individual word choice, the architectural structure of messages—how we sequence information, construct narrative arcs, and deploy rhetorical devices—fundamentally determines persuasive effectiveness. A sales presentation that opens with product features typically generates less customer engagement than one that begins with customer pain points, even when it covers the duplicate content. Legal arguments that front-load their strongest evidence produce different jury deliberations than those that build gradually toward climactic revelations. The grammar of persuasion matters as profoundly as its vocabulary. This chapter explores the granular linguistic mechanics that separate forgettable messages from those that change minds, examining how masterful communicators exploit language's inherent properties to maximum persuasive effect.

The Framing Effect: Linguistic Containers for Ideas

Every message arrives packaged in linguistic frames that profoundly influence interpretation before audiences consciously evaluate content. Farming operates as the conceptual scaffolding that structures how we understand information, determining what aspects become salient and what interpretive schemas audiences apply. When political leaders describe taxation as "revenue investment in collective infrastructure" versus "government confiscation of personal earnings," they're not offering different factual claims—they're establishing radically different interpretive frameworks that make certain aspects visible while rendering others invisible. The frame precedes and shapes content evaluation, functioning as a perceptual filter that determines what audiences even recognize as relevant information.

Cognitive linguist George Lakoff's research on conceptual metaphors reveals that frames operate largely unconsciously, activating entire networks of associated concepts and values. His analysis of political discourse shows how the "strict father" versus "nurturant parent" frames for government create fundamentally different expectations about appropriate policy. Once activated, frames resist revision; attempting to negate a frame often paradoxically reinforces it. When political opponents declare "we're not in a recession," the denial itself activates recession-related conceptual networks. Effective persuaders recognize this dynamic, carefully selecting frame that naturally supports their positions rather than fighting against frames their opponents have established.

Strategic frame selection requires understanding of how different linguistic containers activate different value systems and decision criteria. Environmental advocates learned this lesson through decades of messaging evolution. Early campaigns framed conservation as "sacrifice for future generations," activating frames around duty and delayed gratification. When this proved insufficiently motivating, strategists reframed environmental action as "energy independence and economic opportunity," tapping into entirely different value networks around autonomy and prosperity. The factual content—descriptions of renewable energy technologies, pollution-reduction methods, and policy proposal remained largely consistent. What transformed was the interpretive frame, changing which audience values became relevant to processing the information.

The framing power of language extends into the microstructures of message construction. Research by psychologist Amos Tversky demonstrated that describing medical treatments in terms of "survival rates" versus "mortality rates" significantly altered patient preferences, even when the numbers conveyed identical information. This framing effect appears across diverse domains. Consumers perceive products labeled "95% fat-free" more favorably than identical products labeled "5% fat," even though the products are mathematically equivalent. Job candidates presenting employment gaps as "personal development periods" elicit different responses from interviewers than those describing identical intervals as "unemployment." The frame precedes the content, establishing the evaluative criteria that audiences apply before consciously analyzing information.

Masterful persuaders construct frames proactively rather than reactively, establishing interpretive containers before opponents can impose alternative frameworks. Trial attorneys understand this instinctively, using opening statements to frame case narratives in terms favorable to their clients before jurors hear evidence. A defense attorney might frame a case as "about whether circumstantial evidence reaches the high bar of proof beyond a reasonable doubt." In contrast, prosecutors frame identical proceedings as "about justice for victims and community safety." Both frames are technically accurate, but each directs attention toward different evidence and activates different values. The attorney who establishes the dominant frame typically prevails, regardless of subsequent argumentation quality. This reveals a crucial truth about linguistic persuasion: controlling the frame often matters more than maintaining the facts.

Semantic Precision and Strategic Ambiguity

Effective persuasive language navigates a sophisticated balance between precision and ambiguity, knowing when crystal clarity serves persuasive goals and when productive vagueness opens possibilities. Conventional wisdom suggests that clear, specific language always strengthens messages, but persuasion research reveals a more nuanced reality. Sometimes, semantic precision constrains message appeal by forcing audiences into binary acceptance or rejection. Strategic ambiguity, conversely, allows diverse audiences to project their own interpretations onto messages, finding personal relevance and meaning without requiring universal agreement on specifics.

Political rhetoric exemplifies this dynamic. When leaders declare commitments to "family values" or "economic opportunity," the deliberate vagueness allows coalition-building across constituencies who might disagree on policy specifics. Conservative and progressive voters interpret "family values" through different conceptual frameworks, yet both can endorse the general principle. This strategic ambiguity isn't mere evasiveness—it's sophisticated recognition that premature precision can foreclose persuasive possibilities. Once a politician specifies precisely which family configurations embody "proper values," half the potential coalition is likely to defect. The ambiguous formulation maintains big-tent appeal while signaling general priorities.

However, persuaders must recognize contexts where ambiguity undermines credibility, and precision enhances persuasive power. Technical and professional contexts typically demand semantic precision. When engineers propose infrastructure projects, vague references to "improved safety" lack the compelling force of specific metrics: "reducing accident frequency by thirty-seven percent based on traffic flow modeling." Medical professionals explaining treatment options must provide precise information about success rates, side effects, and recovery timelines; ambiguity here generates anxiety rather than comfort. Financial advisors who speak vaguely about "strong returns" sacrifice credibility compared to those offering specific performance projections with clearly articulated assumptions and risk parameters.

The precision-ambiguity balance also varies across persuasive message stages. Early in persuasive campaigns, strategic ambiguity often attracts broad interest and minimizes premature rejection. A nonprofit launching a community health initiative might initially promote vague goals around "wellness and vitality" to build diverse stakeholder coalitions. As the campaign progresses, increasingly specific language becomes necessary—precise program descriptions, detailed outcome metrics, explicit resource requirements. The progression from strategic ambiguity to semantic precision mirrors the audience's evolving relationship with the proposal, providing appropriate information density for each engagement stage.

Skilled persuaders also recognize that specific linguistic constructions create productive ambiguity through pronoun use and passive voice. Consider the difference between "we must reform this system" and "the system requires reform." The second formulation depersonalizes agencies, potentially reducing defensiveness among those implicated in current practices while still advocating change. Similarly, strategic pronoun shifting—moving between "I," "we," "you," and "one" allows persuaders to adjust psychological distance. "You need to consider alternative perspectives" sounds more confrontational than "one should consider alternative perspectives," which conveys a similar directive force with less interpersonal pressure. These subtle linguistic mechanisms offer tools for managing the precision-ambiguity spectrum at grammatical levels beyond mere word choice.

Linguistic Devices: Rhythm, Repetition, and Rhetorical Flourish

Language possesses inherent musical qualities that enhance or undermine persuasive impact independent of semantic content. The rhythm of sentences, the cadence of delivery, and the sonic properties of word sequences influence message processing and memorability. Effective persuaders exploit these acoustic dimensions, recognizing that audiences experience messages not merely as information transmission but as linguistic performance. A proposal delivered in choppy, irregular sentences generates different cognitive responses than identical content arranged in flowing, rhythmic prose—the music of language matters.

Rhetorical repetition—dismissed by writing instructors as redundancy—serves crucial persuasive functions when deployed strategically. Anaphora —the repetition of words or phrases at clause beginnings —creates rhythmic momentum while emphasizing key concepts. Winston Churchill's famous declaration, "We shall fight on the beaches, we shall fight on the landing grounds, we shall fight in the fields and in the streets," demonstrates how repetition transforms simple determination into rhetorical inevitability. Each repeated "we shall fight" pounds the message deeper into the audience's consciousness, building a cumulative force that a single statement cannot achieve. Repetition isn't wasteful; it's architecturally essential to the message's psychological impact.

Parallel structure—maintaining grammatical consistency across related phrases—eases cognitive processing, enhancing message comprehension. Compare "Our organization values innovation, people who collaborate, and integrity" with "Our organization values innovation, collaboration, and integrity." The second version's parallel noun structure reduces cognitive load, allowing audiences to process the series effortlessly. This grammatical harmony signals organizational thinking and professionalism while making content more memorable. Abraham Lincoln's "government of the people, by the people, for the people" derives rhetorical power partly from its perfect parallel structure, which makes the phrase sonically satisfying and cognitively sticky.

Alliteration and assonance—repetition of consonant and vowel sounds—create sonic cohesion that aids recall and signals message craftsmanship. Marketing slogans exploit this principle extensively: "Coca-Cola," "Best Buy," "Dunkin' Donuts," "PayPal." The sound patterns make brand names more phonetically pleasing and memorable. Political speechwriters employ similar techniques: "compassionate conservatism," "tough on crime," "bridge to the future." These phrases possess sonic integrity that makes them easier to process cognitively and reproduce, increasing their memetic potential. When audiences can easily remember and repeat messages, persuasive impact extends beyond initial exposure.

Rhetorical questions serve as a persuasive function by engaging audiences in quasi-dialogic interaction. Rather than declaratively stating "This approach won't work," asking "How could this approach possibly succeed given current constraints?" invites audiences into collaborative problem-solving while directing them toward predetermined conclusions. The question format appears to respect audience autonomy—you're asking rather than telling—while subtly guiding thinking. Skilled persuaders deploy questions to surface concerns they'll subsequently address, creating the perception that their messages respond to audience needs rather than imposing predetermined agendas.

The persuasive power of concrete, sensory language surpasses abstract formulations even when describing identical concepts. Research by cognitive scientists demonstrates that concrete language activates more neural regions than abstract terminology, creating richer mental representations. Compare "We need improved operational efficiency" with "We need to eliminate the three-hour delays customers currently experience when requesting service appointments." The concrete version triggers mental imagery—frustrated customers, ticking clocks, appointment calendars—that abstract "efficiency" cannot. This sensory richness increases message salience and memorability. Effective persuaders systematically convert abstract concepts into concrete scenarios, recognizing that vivid particulars persuade more effectively than bloodless generalizations.

The Architecture of Narrative: Storytelling as Persuasive Structure

Human cognition exhibits deep structural affinity for narrative form, making story-based messages neurologically privileged compared to other information presentation modes. Neuroscientific research reveals that narratives activate multiple brain regions simultaneously—not merely language-processing areas but also the motor cortex (when stories describe action), sensory regions (when narratives include sensory details), and emotional centers (when characters encounter meaningful experiences). This neural coupling creates immersive processing experiences where audiences mentally simulate story events, generating engagement levels impossible through abstract argumentation alone. Masterful persuaders exploit narrative's neurological advantages by embedding proposals within story structures.

Compelling, persuasive narratives require specific architectural elements that distinguish coherent stories from mere chronological reporting. Story structure demands identifiable characters facing meaningful challenges, attempting solutions, and experiencing consequences. A nonprofit director seeking funding who recounts program activities" we served 500 families, conducted 20 workshops, distributed 1000 resource packets"—provides information without narrative. Contrast this with: "Maria arrived at our center having fled domestic violence with her three children and $40 in cash. Over six months, our housing program helped her secure safe accommodation, our job training enabled her to earn her medical assistant certification, and our childcare supported her employment search. Maria now earns $42,000 annually and recently made her first month's rent payment from her own earnings." The second version constructs a narrative with a protagonist, obstacle, intervention, and resolution—a story architecture that engages audiences emotionally and cognitively in ways that data recitation cannot.

The persuasive power of narrative extends beyond emotional engagement to include transportation, the psychological phenomenon where audiences become cognitively absorbed in stories, suspending critical evaluation. Communication researcher Melanie Green's studies demonstrate that transported audiences show reduced counterarguing and greater attitude change than those processing identical information in non-narrative formats. When audiences experience transportation, they enter the story world rather than maintaining analytical distance. This cognitive immersion creates persuasive opportunities because transported audiences process story implications as lived experiences rather than external claims requiring skeptical evaluation. Embedding proposals within compelling narratives effectively reduces psychological resistance.

Strategic narrative construction requires understanding which story elements maximize persuasive impact. Character identification—audiences seeing themselves or aspirational versions of themselves in story protagonists—strengthens narrative persuasion. Healthcare providers promoting preventive care might feature relatable patients whose early screening detected treatable conditions rather than emphasizing abstract statistics about detection rates. The relatable character offers opportunities for identification, making audiences think "that could be me" rather than "those are interesting numbers." Similarly, narrative specificity—concrete details about settings, emotions, and sensory experiences—enhances transportation by enabling audiences to construct vivid mental simulations. Generic descriptions ("a patient benefited from early treatment") lack the immersive power of specific narratives ("James noticed persistent fatigue during his morning runs, mentioned it during his annual physical, and discovered Stage 1 lymphoma that responded completely to six months of treatment").

However, persuaders must calibrate narrative intensity to avoid overwhelming cognitive capacity or triggering defensive responses. Overly dramatic narratives can activate skepticism rather than transportation, particularly when audiences perceive emotional manipulation. Research on narrative persuasion suggests that moderately dramatic stories often persuade more effectively than extreme examples because audiences find them more plausible and representative. A financial planning firm might achieve greater persuasive impact by describing a client who retired comfortably through consistent saving rather than featuring someone who became a multi-millionaire through savvy investments. The moderate narrative feels achievable and relevant, while the extreme version might trigger dismissal: "That's not realistic for someone like me."

The conclusion of persuasive narratives carries disproportionate weight because story endings shape retrospective interpretation of all preceding events. Narratives concluding with ambiguity or adverse outcomes rarely serve persuasive goals unless explicitly designed to motivate problem-solving or prevention. More commonly, compelling persuasive narratives conclude with a resolution that demonstrates the benefits of the proposed actions or attitudes. This doesn't require unrealistic positivity— complex, qualified resolutions can work effectively—but audiences need clear takeaways about why the narrative matters for their own decision-making. The story ending should organically illuminate the message's core persuasive claim without heavy-handed moralizing that ruptures narrative immersion and reactivates analytical resistance.

Metaphorical Thinking: Concept Mapping Through Language

Metaphor functions as far more than decorative language—it constitutes a fundamental cognitive mechanism through which humans understand abstract concepts by mapping them onto more concrete, embodied experiences. When we describe arguments as "strong" or "weak," we understand time as something we "spend" or "save," or conceptualize ideas as "grasping" or "reaching beyond our grasp," we're using metaphorical mappings that structure cognition itself. Persuaders who skillfully deploy metaphors don't merely add linguistic flourish; they actively shape the conceptual frameworks that audiences use to understand proposals and make decisions.

Different metaphors for identical phenomena generate radically different implications and action tendencies. Consider metaphorical variations for describing organizational challenges. Framing a problem as a "roadblock" suggests something that obstructs forward progress and requires removal or circumvention. The same situation, described as "quicksand," implies danger of continued movement and a need for careful, measured responses. Characterizing it as "a puzzle" frames the challenge as intellectually engaging with solutions discoverable through clever thinking. Each metaphor carries distinct implications about the nature of the problem, appropriate responses, and probable outcomes. Persuaders selecting metaphors effectively predetermine much of how audiences will think about issues.

Extended metaphors—sustained conceptual mappings developed throughout messages—create compelling, persuasive frameworks. When business leaders describe organizations as "organisms" that must "evolve" or "adapt" to "survive" in competitive "ecosystems," they've activated an entire biological framework that makes confident strategic choices appear natural. In contrast, others seem contrary to organizational survival. This organic metaphor differs fundamentally from describing organizations as "machines" requiring "efficiency," "optimization," and "precision engineering." The machine metaphor privileges different values and action tendencies than the organism metaphor, demonstrating how sustained metaphorical frameworks shape strategic thinking and decision criteria.

However, metaphors also constrain thinking by making certain aspects salient while obscuring others. The "war on drugs" metaphor frames substance abuse as an enemy requiring military-style combat, emphasizing enforcement and punishment while de-emphasizing public health approaches. This metaphorical frame dominated policy for decades, creating intellectual path dependency that made alternative approaches difficult to conceptualize. Persuaders introducing new metaphorical frames face the challenge of dislodging entrenched conceptual mappings. Contemporary reformers attempting to reframe substance issues through "treatment" and "recovery" metaphors must overcome the cognitive momentum of military metaphors that shaped policy and public understanding for generations.

Cross-cultural persuasion requires particular attention to metaphorical variation because cultures employ different conceptual mappings for fundamental experiences. Time metaphors illustrate this variation dramatically. English speakers predominantly conceptualize time as moving horizontally ("looking forward to the future," "putting the past behind us"), while Mandarin speakers commonly use vertical time metaphors ("previous month" literally translates as "up month," "next month" as "down month"). These differing metaphorical systems aren't mere linguistic curiosities—they shape cognition about temporal relationships and causality. Persuaders working across cultural contexts must recognize that metaphors that carry intuitive force in one cultural framework may confuse or mislead audiences operating within different metaphorical systems.

The most effective persuasive metaphors connect abstract concepts to embodied physical experiences that audiences universally understand. Temperature metaphors for emotional states ("warm relationship," "cold reception," "heated argument") work across cultures because all humans' experience temperature somatically. Similarly, metaphors grounded in spatial relationships ("high status," "low morale," "rising above challenges") leverage universal human experiences of verticality and its ties to effort and value.

Persuaders selecting metaphors with universal experiential bases create conceptual bridges that facilitate understanding across diverse audiences, while overly culture-specific metaphors risk confusion or misinterpretation.

Linguistic Subtlety: Implicature and Indirect Speech

Explicit directness represents only one mode of linguistic persuasion; often, indirect communication achieves impossible effects through blunt statement. Pragmatic implicature—meaning conveyed indirectly through contextual interpretation rather than literal semantic content—allows persuaders to suggest ideas while maintaining plausible deniability and reducing audience reactance. When a supervisor tells an underperforming employee, "I'm sure you want to succeed here," it's merely a form of reassurance. The pragmatic implicature—"your current performance threatens your position and must improve"—communicates forcefully without confronting the recipient, which might trigger defensiveness. This linguistic indirection serves crucial social and persuasive functions.

The theory of conversational implicature, developed by philosopher Paul Grice, explains how audiences derive implied meanings by assuming communicators follow cooperative principles: relevance (contributions relate to ongoing conversation), quantity (providing appropriate information levels), quality (truthfulness), and manner (clarity and orderliness). When speakers apparently violate these principles, audiences infer that the conveyed meaning differs from the literal content. A job candidate who responds, "I'm very detail-oriented," to a question about weaknesses appears to violate relevance by not directly addressing the question. Skilled interviewers recognize this as implicating "I have no significant weaknesses I'm willing to discuss," understanding that the apparent violation signals intentional indirection.

Indirect speech serves particularly important functions when addressing status differences or making socially delicate requests. Research by psychologist Steven Pinker demonstrates that indirect formulations maintain social relationships while accomplishing transactional goals. "Would you be willing to write a recommendation letter?" preserves the recipient's autonomy and allows a graceful refusal, whereas "Write me a recommendation letter." would not. The indirect formulation achieves the request while acknowledging the recipient's agency and the speaker's awareness that compliance isn't obligatory. This social lubrication makes indirect requests paradoxically more effective than direct demands in many contexts, even though they require more words and create temporary ambiguity.

Euphemism represents another form of linguistic indirection serving persuasive purposes. Describing employee termination as "rightsizing" or "transitioning roles" softens harsh realities through semantic distance. While critics dismiss euphemism as deceptive obfuscation, pragmatic analysis reveals more nuanced functions. Euphemisms can demonstrate sensitivity to emotional impact while still conveying necessary information. Medical professionals describing "negative outcomes" rather than "deaths" aren't necessarily obscuring facts but managing the emotional intensity of communications with grieving families. Euphemistic indirection shows awareness of psychological impact while fulfilling informational obligations. Context determines whether euphemism serves considerate communication or deceptive manipulation.

However, excessive indirection risks communication failure when audiences don't share sufficient contextual knowledge to derive implied meanings. Cross-cultural persuasion is particularly vulnerable to implicature failures because cultural groups develop different conventions regarding the appropriateness of directness and implicature interpretation. High-context cultures (including many Asian and Middle Eastern societies) rely heavily on indirect communication, with much of the meaning conveyed through contextual interpretation. Low-context cultures (including most Western societies) prefer explicit, direct communication, viewing indirection as vague or potentially dishonest. Persuaders working across cultural contexts must calibrate their levels of indirection appropriately, recognizing that strategies effective in one cultural framework may confuse or alienate audiences from different communicative traditions.

The persuasive power of linguistic craftsmanship ultimately derives from recognizing that language doesn't merely describe reality—it actively constructs the experiential and conceptual frameworks through which audiences encounter ideas. Every word selected, every metaphor deployed, every narrative structure chosen shapes how audiences think about proposals and make decisions. Masterful persuaders approach language as architects rather than mere decorators, carefully constructing messages that guide audiences toward desired conclusions while respecting their autonomy and intelligence. Power resides not in manipulation but in a sophisticated understanding of how linguistic choices shape human cognition and behavior. Words don't just matter— they create the worlds within which persuasion succeeds or fails.

Chapter 4: Emotional Appeals: Connecting with the Heart

When a museum curator decides which photograph to display at the entrance of a Holocaust memorial, she understands that her selection will determine whether visitors enter with intellectual detachment or visceral emotional engagement. When a defense attorney chooses whether to introduce testimony from a defendant's elderly mother during closing arguments, he recognizes that this decision may influence the jury more powerfully than any forensic evidence. When a conservation organization debates whether to feature starving polar bears or thriving wildlife sanctuaries in its campaign, it acknowledges that emotional resonance often determines donation behavior more than scientific data on carbon emissions. These moments illuminate a fundamental truth about persuasion: human beings make decisions with their hearts and subsequently rationalize those decisions with their minds. Understanding how to connect with audiences at an emotional level authentically represents perhaps the most potent yet ethically complex dimension of persuasive communication.

The landscape of emotional persuasion extends far beyond simple sentiment or manipulation. It encompasses a sophisticated understanding of psychological vulnerabilities, cultural values, personal identity, and the neurobiological substrates that generate feeling states. Modern affective neuroscience reveals that emotion and cognition do not operate as separate systems but rather function as deeply integrated networks in which feeling states influence information processing at every level. Damage to emotional processing centers in the brain, as neurologist Antonio Damasio's research with patients suffering ventromedial prefrontal cortex lesions demonstrates, doesn't produce hyperrational decision-makers but rather individuals who become paralyzed by choice, unable to commit to even trivial decisions. This neurological reality suggests that emotion serves not as reason's enemy but as its essential partner, providing the value judgments and priority weightings that make decision-making possible. Effective emotional appeals don't bypass rational thought; instead, they engage the emotional systems that enable and direct cognitive processing toward meaningful conclusions.

The ethical dimensions of emotional persuasion generate considerable debate among communication scholars, practitioners, and critics. Some argue that emotional appeals inherently manipulate audiences by exploiting psychological vulnerabilities rather than engaging rational faculties. Others contend that emotion represents a legitimate and essential component of human experience that deserves recognition in persuasive discourse. This tension reflects more profound philosophical questions about human nature, autonomy, and the relationship between feeling and thinking. The position advanced here recognizes that emotional appeals become ethically problematic not through their existence but through their execution. Deceptive emotional manipulation—deliberately triggering fear or compassion through fabricated scenarios—clearly violates ethical boundaries. However, authentic emotional appeals that help audiences connect intellectual understanding to personal meaning serve a legitimate function: making abstract information psychologically real. The pediatrician who describes not just the statistics about vaccination effectiveness but also her experience watching previously healthy children suffer from preventable diseases engages in ethical emotional persuasion by providing context that helps parents make informed decisions rather than merely processing abstract probability calculations.

The Emotional Gradient: Beyond Simple Positive and Negative Affect

Understanding emotional appeals requires moving beyond simplistic categorizations of positive versus negative emotions to recognize the nuanced spectrum of specific feeling states that different persuasive contexts demand. Psychologist Robert Plutchik's emotion wheel identifies eight primary emotions—joy, trust, fear, surprise, sadness, disgust, anger, and anticipation—that combine and vary in intensity to create the full richness of human emotional experience. Each emotional state creates a distinct psychological readiness for particular types of messages and actions. Fear heightens vigilance and motivates protective behaviors, making it effective for public health warnings or security messaging but potentially counterproductive when it generates defensive avoidance rather than constructive engagement. Anger energizes action and breaks through complacency, which explains its prevalence in social justice movements and political campaigns; yet excessive anger can overwhelm rational evaluation and promote destructive rather than constructive responses.

The emotion of elevation, identified by psychologist Jonathan Haidt, represents a particularly potent but underutilized persuasive tool. Elevation occurs when witnessing acts of moral beauty, compassion, or exceptional virtue, generating a warm feeling in the chest, tears of admiration, and motivation to become a better person. Charity organizations that share stories of extreme generosity—a teacher donating a kidney to a student, a community rallying to rebuild a neighbor's destroyed home— tap into the unique power of elevation. Unlike guilt-based appeals, which often trigger defensive responses, elevation creates approach motivation, leading audiences to align with the moral excellence they've witnessed. The feeling doesn't demand self-flagellation about personal inadequacy but rather inspires aspiration toward perceived goodness. This emotional dynamic explains why narrative campaigns featuring extraordinary altruism often outperform statistical presentations of need, even though the latter might seem more rationally compelling. The elevation response bypasses cognitive resistance mechanisms precisely because it doesn't feel like persuasion at all but rather like inspiration.

Nostalgia presents another sophisticated emotional appeal that operates through complex psychological mechanisms beyond simple sentimentality. When political campaigns invoke bygone eras of national prosperity, when brands resurrect vintage packaging designs, when retirement communities emphasize continuity with residents' personal histories, they leverage nostalgia's unique properties. Psychological research by Constantine Sedikides demonstrates that nostalgia serves critical regulatory functions: it counteracts loneliness, boredom, and anxiety while boosting self-esteem and social connectedness. Nostalgic memories typically feature the self as protagonist surrounded by close others, creating a sense of meaning and belonging. However, persuaders must navigate nostalgia carefully because it simultaneously creates openness to messages associated with positive memories while potentially generating resistance to change. The retirement community that evokes nostalgia for residents' most vibrant years while implicitly suggesting those years are permanently past may inadvertently trigger depression rather than engagement. More effective nostalgic appeals connect past experiences to present possibilities, using memory as a bridge rather than a destination. The campaign that reminds voters of community solidarity during historical challenges while advocating for contemporary collective action leverages nostalgia productively rather than regressively.

The emotion of hope deserves particular attention because it occupies unique territory in the persuasive landscape. Unlike optimism, which reflects a general disposition toward positive expectations, hope emerges specifically in challenging circumstances where positive outcomes remain possible but uncertain. Psychologist Charles Snyder's hope theory identifies two essential components: agency (the belief in one's capacity to act) and pathways (perceptions of viable routes to desired goals). Persuasive messages that cultivate hope must therefore provide both empowerment and direction. Environmental campaigns face this challenge acutely: messages emphasizing climate catastrophe without offering meaningful action pathways that generate despair and disengagement rather than behavioral change. More effective approaches acknowledge legitimate concerns while highlighting specific, achievable actions that contribute to solutions. The key distinction lies between false hope that overpromises easy solutions and authentic hope that recognizes difficulty while maintaining possibility. When medical professionals communicate with patients facing serious diagnoses, those who skillfully balance realistic assessment with hope facilitate better psychological adjustment and even improved health outcomes compared to those who either minimize difficulties or eliminate hope through excessive pessimism.

Emotional Contagion and Social Proof in Collective Decision-Making

Human beings possess remarkable capacities for emotional contagion—automatically mimicking and subsequently experiencing emotions observed in others. This phenomenon operates through mirror neuron systems that fire both when we experience emotions directly and when we perceive emotional expressions in others. The implications for persuasion are profound: audiences don't merely observe persuaders' emotional states; they unconsciously simulate and adopt them. The nonprofit fundraiser who radiates genuine warmth and compassion while discussing organizational mission creates emotional resonance beyond the content of her words. Conversely, the sales professional whose anxiety about meeting quotas manifests as subtle tension cues triggers unease in prospects, regardless of product merit. This neurological reality means persuaders must cultivate authentic emotional states rather than merely perform emotional displays, as audiences possess sophisticated, largely unconscious capacities to detect emotional authenticity.

The dynamics of emotional contagion amplify dramatically in group contexts where multiple individuals simultaneously experience and express emotions. Research on collective effervescence, the sensation of energized unity that emerges during shared emotional experiences—reveals how group settings transform individual emotional experiences into powerful collective phenomena. Religious gatherings, political rallies, concerts, and sporting events all leverage collective effervescence to create memorable experiences that strengthen group identification and commitment. Persuaders operating in group contexts can either harness these dynamics productively or fall victim to them. The conference speaker who begins with vulnerability about personal struggles and subsequently observes audience members visibly moved, some nodding or wiping tears, has initiated emotional contagion, creating receptivity to subsequent messages. The emotional connection established precedes and enables the cognitive content that follows. However, emotional contagion in groups can also spread negative states: anxiety, skepticism, or hostility that begins with one or two individuals can rapidly proliferate through emotional mimicry, undermining persuasive efforts before they fully develop.

Understanding emotional social proof—the tendency to validate one's emotional responses by observing others' emotional reactions—adds another layer to group persuasion dynamics. Individuals often feel uncertain about how to respond emotionally to ambiguous situations and look to others for cues on appropriate reactions. Canned laughter in television comedies, though universally recognized as artificial, continues to increase viewer amusement because it provides social proof that laughter represents the proper response. In persuasive contexts, this means that visible emotional reactions from some audience members influence how others experience and evaluate messages. The job candidate who observes interview committee members smiling and leaning forward gains confidence that manifests in improved performance, creating a positive feedback loop. Conversely, the presenter who notices skeptical expressions may become defensive, undermining message effectiveness. Sophisticated persuaders recognize these dynamics and sometimes employ strategies to seed desired emotional responses: placing supportive individuals strategically in the audience, featuring testimonials that model desired emotional reactions, or creating interactive elements that invite emotional expression from receptive participants, whose responses then influence others.

The Narrative Transportation Theory: Emotion Through Story

While previous chapters addressed various persuasive dimensions, the specific mechanism of narrative transportation—the phenomenon where audiences become cognitively and emotionally absorbed into story worlds—represents a distinct emotional persuasion pathway worthy of deep exploration. Psychologists Melanie Green and Timothy Brock developed narrative transportation theory to explain why stories often persuade more effectively than statistical evidence or logical arguments. Transportation occurs when audience members lose awareness of their immediate surroundings, become focused on story events, experience vivid mental imagery of story elements, and generate emotional responses to characters' experiences. During high transportation, audiences temporarily suspend critical evaluation mechanisms, become less aware of persuasive intent, and prove more receptive to story-embedded messages.

The neurological underpinnings of narrative transportation reveal why stories generate such robust emotional responses. When we read or hear stories, our brains don't simply process linguistic information abstractly but simulate the experiences described. If a character runs, our motor cortex activates; if a character feels heartbreak, our emotional processing centers engage; if a character faces moral dilemmas, our regions associated with theory of mind and ethical reasoning show increased activity. This neural simulation creates vicarious experiences that feel psychologically real even while we consciously recognize them as fictional. The implications for persuasion prove profound: through narrative transportation, audiences can experience consequences, emotions, and insights they've never encountered directly. The documentary filmmaker who shares an immigrant family's journey creates understanding that statistical immigration data cannot match because audiences don't merely learn about experiences—they simulate living them. The emotional investment generated by transportation transforms audiences from detached evaluators into engaged participants, whose identities and values become entangled with the story elements.

However, narrative transportation's persuasive power depends critically on the quality of story construction. Poorly crafted narratives that strain credibility, feature implausible character motivations, or employ heavy-handed messaging disrupt transportation, returning audiences to critical evaluation mode. The commercial that tells an emotionally manipulative story culminating in an obvious product pitch triggers recognition of persuasive intent that eliminates transportation benefits. More effective approaches embed persuasive elements organically within compelling narratives where emotional engagement precedes and outlasts explicit persuasive content. Consider pharmaceutical companies that share patient stories in advocacy campaigns. The most effective narratives focus on patients lived experiences—the practical challenges of managing conditions, the emotional impact on relationships, the meaning of restored functionality—without emphasizing pharmaceutical products until late in the narrative, if at all. The emotional connection established through transportation creates generalized receptivity to subsequent messages that would otherwise encounter skepticism in direct appeals. The audience member, emotionally transported by a patient's struggle, subsequently proves more receptive to information about treatment options because the emotional investment generated by the story makes solutions feel personally relevant rather than commercially motivated.

Strategic Emotional Sequencing: Creating Persuasive Emotional Journeys

Sophisticated emotional persuasion rarely relies on single emotional appeals but rather orchestrates emotional sequences that guide audiences through deliberately constructed affective journeys. The documentary filmmaker Ken Burns exemplifies this approach in his historical narratives, which typically begin with curiosity and interest, build through revelation and surprise as hidden stories emerge, intensify through moral indignation or sorrow as injustices or tragedies unfold, and resolve through inspiration as individuals demonstrate courage or resilience. This emotional architecture serves persuasive functions beyond entertainment value. Progression creates psychological investment that makes abandoning the narrative costly, builds emotional energy that peaks strategically at moments of key messaging, and concludes with feelings that motivate desired actions or perspective shifts.

The principle of emotional contrast amplifies persuasive impact by juxtaposing opposing emotional states. Charity campaigns frequently employ contrast by presenting dire circumstances followed by transformation enabled through intervention. The viewer first experiences distress observing suffering, then relief and hope witnessing recovery, creating an emotional range that makes the impact tangible. This sequencing proves more effective than sustained negative emotion, which generates defense mechanisms and disengagement, or sustained positive emotion, which lacks urgency and fails to demonstrate need. The emotional contrast provides both motivation (alleviating suffering) and reward (experiencing transformation), creating complete persuasive architecture. Similarly, corporate change management initiatives often sequence emotions strategically: acknowledgment of legitimate frustrations with current systems generates validation and trust, followed by excitement about future possibilities that create motivation, concluding with confidence through detailed implementation plans that reduce anxiety. This emotional progression addresses the full spectrum of psychological needs that change initiatives trigger.

The closing emotional note deserves strategic attention because of recency effects in memory and the powerful influence of endings on overall experience evaluation. Psychologist Daniel Kahneman's research on the peak-end rule demonstrates that people evaluate experiences primarily based on emotional intensity peaks and final moments rather than average emotion throughout. This finding suggests that persuaders should carefully architect the emotional states that follow, rather than let them end when the content concludes. The speech that ends with quiet inspiration rather than fading anticlimactically, the sales presentation that concludes with client excitement rather than logistical details, the therapy session that finishes with hope and empowerment rather than unresolved distress—all leverage strategic emotional sequencing to maximize persuasive impact. However, this requires moving beyond formulaic emotional manipulation to a genuine understanding of audiences' emotional needs and an authentic commitment to meeting them. The defense attorney who saves her most emotionally powerful testimony for closing arguments doesn't manipulate cynically; instead, she recognizes that jurors need emotional closure as much as logical summation. The emotional journey she constructs serves both rhetorical effectiveness and psychological completion.

Cultural Dimensions of Emotional Persuasion

Emotional appeals that resonate powerfully in one cultural context may fail or backfire in another because cultures differ dramatically in emotional norms, expression rules, and the relationship between feeling and acting. Psychologist David Matsumoto's research on display rules—cultural norms governing when, how, and to whom emotions should be expressed—reveals substantial cross-cultural variation. High-context cultures that emphasize social harmony and indirect communication often view overt emotional displays as inappropriate or unsophisticated. The sales approach that succeeds in the United States through enthusiasm and emotional expressiveness may alienate Japanese clients who interpret such displays as lacking professional restraint. Conversely, the measured, understated approach that demonstrates respect in many Asian cultures may strike American audiences as disengaged or untrustworthy.

Cultural differences extend beyond expression to emotional concepts themselves. The German idea of *Schadenfreude* (pleasure derived from others' misfortune), the Japanese *amae* (dependence on and presumption of another's benevolence), or the Portuguese *saudade* (melancholic longing tinged with hope)—these culture-specific emotions lack direct equivalents in other languages because they reflect unique cultural values and social structures. Persuaders working across cultures must recognize that emotional appeals leveraging culture-specific emotions prove untranslatable. Marketing campaigns that assume universal emotional categories often fail because they miss culturally specific resonances that create persuasive power. The advertisement evoking nostalgic family gatherings around foods works brilliantly when targeting cultures with strong food-centered family traditions, but falls flat elsewhere. More fundamentally, cultures differ in whether emotional appeals themselves are considered legitimate persuasive tools. Societies emphasizing rationality and individual autonomy may view emotional persuasion skeptically as manipulation, while cultures prioritizing relationship harmony and collective welfare may consider emotion essential to authentic communication.

The cultural dimension of emotional intensity proves particularly critical. Mediterranean cultures generally embrace high emotional expressiveness as authentic communication, while Northern European cultures often value emotional restraint as a marker of maturity and professionalism. These differences create cross-cultural persuasion challenges: the Italian entrepreneur whose passionate pitch impresses investors in Milan may overwhelm executives in Stockholm, who perceive it as excessive emotionality. Effective cross-cultural persuaders develop emotional code-switching abilities—adjusting the intensity of their emotional expressions to align with cultural expectations while maintaining authenticity. This requires moving beyond surface-level emotional performance to a genuine understanding of cultural emotional logics. The consultant who succeeds internationally doesn't merely modulate volume and gesture; they comprehend how different cultures conceptualize the relationship between emotion and credibility, between feeling and truth, between expressiveness and authenticity. This deeper cultural emotional intelligence enables persuasion that honors local norms while achieving communicative goals.

Emotional Vulnerability as Persuasive Strength

Contemporary research on authentic leadership and therapeutic communication reveals counterintuitive findings about the persuasive power of emotional vulnerability. Traditional persuasion models often assumed that demonstrating strength, confidence, and invulnerability builds credibility and trust. However, psychologist Brené

Brown's research on vulnerability demonstrates that strategic disclosure of authentic emotional struggles, uncertainties, and failures often generates stronger connections and influence than polished presentations of flawless competence. When leaders acknowledge genuine fear about organizational challenges while maintaining a commitment to addressing them, team members report higher trust and a greater willingness to contribute effort than when leaders project unrealistic confidence. This phenomenon operates through multiple psychological mechanisms: vulnerability demonstrates authenticity because emotional perfection signals performance rather than genuine experience; it creates identification as audiences recognize shared human struggles; and it invites reciprocal vulnerability that deepens relationships.

The distinction between strategic vulnerability and emotional oversharing proves critical for persuasive effectiveness. Productive vulnerability involves selective disclosure of authentic emotional experiences relevant to the persuasive context, shared with appropriate boundaries and a clear connection to audience benefit. The political candidate who discusses personal struggles with healthcare access while advocating for policy reform demonstrates strategic vulnerability that creates identification and illustrates policy stakes. The same candidate who extensively discusses marital conflicts or personal insecurities unrelated to governance demonstrates poor boundary management, undermining rather than enhancing credibility. Strategic vulnerability requires self-awareness about which emotional disclosures serve communicative purposes and which merely burden audiences with intimate information they cannot productively use. It also demands emotional regulation skills—the capacity to access and express authentic emotion without becoming overwhelmed by it. The persuader who tears up briefly while discussing meaningful subject matter demonstrates authentic engagement; the persuader who dissolves into uncontrolled sobbing shifts the audience's focus from the message content to caretaking responsibility.

Vulnerability's persuasive impact varies significantly by role and context. Healthcare providers who acknowledge emotional responses to patient suffering while maintaining professional composure often develop stronger therapeutic relationships than those who remain completely detached. Teachers who admit when they don't know the answers while demonstrating a commitment to learning alongside students usually inspire deeper engagement than those who pretend to know it all. However, vulnerability carries different risks and rewards depending on power dynamics. Leaders disclosing vulnerability from positions of established authority typically gain trust because they could maintain facades but choose authenticity. The same vulnerability from individuals lacking credibility or status may reinforce perceptions of weakness rather than building a connection. This reality creates persuasive dilemmas for marginalized groups who must balance the relational benefits of vulnerability against risks of confirming negative stereotypes. Women leaders who share emotional experiences may face backlash rooted in gender stereotypes that men who express the same emotions avoid. Understanding when vulnerability serves persuasive goals versus when it exposes communicators to prejudicial evaluation requires sophisticated social awareness and strategic judgment that extends beyond simple authenticity promotion.

The landscape of emotional persuasion encompasses far more than this chapter can fully explore, yet the principles examined here provide essential foundations for ethical and effective emotional engagement. Recognizing emotion as legitimate rather than manipulative, understanding the distinct psychological functions of specific emotional states, orchestrating emotional sequences strategically, honoring cultural differences, and embracing authentic vulnerability when appropriate—these capabilities transform emotional persuasion from crude manipulation into sophisticated communication that honors both persuasive goals and audience humanity. The persuader who connects genuinely with hearts while simultaneously engaging minds creates a lasting influence that mere logical argument or emotional manipulation alone cannot achieve. This integration of emotional wisdom with communicative skill represents not persuasion's enemy but its highest expression, where influence serves not just immediate goals but builds the trust and understanding that makes sustained relationships and meaningful social cooperation possible.

Chapter 5: The Role of Credibility and Trust

When Johnson & Johnson faced the Tylenol poisoning crisis in 1982, seven people had died from tampered capsules laced with cyanide. The company stood at a precipice where a single miscalculation could obliterate decades of accumulated trust. Their decision to immediately recall 31 million bottles—costing over $100 million—defied conventional business logic focused on minimizing liability and protecting quarterly earnings. Yet within months, Tylenol had regained market leadership, and J&J's reputation had paradoxically strengthened. This counterintuitive outcome reveals a fundamental principle of persuasion that transcends communication techniques or rhetorical skill: when credibility and trust form the foundation of influence, decisions that sacrifice short-term gains to preserve that foundation are the most strategically sound investments a persuader can make. The company didn't merely survive a crisis; they demonstrated that authentic trustworthiness constitutes a form of capital more valuable than any immediate financial consideration.

Understanding credibility and trust requires moving beyond simplistic definitions that treat these concepts as mere personality traits or communication add-ons. Credibility represents the audience's assessment of whether a persuader possesses the qualifications, expertise, and reliability necessary to warrant serious consideration of their claims. Trust constitutes something more profound: the willingness to make oneself vulnerable based on positive expectations about another's intentions and future behavior. A cardiac surgeon gains credibility through medical credentials and surgical outcomes; patients trust that surgeon when they consent to anesthesia, temporarily relinquishing consciousness and control over their own survival. This distinction matters because persuasion frequently requires asking audiences to accept risk—whether adopting untested business strategies, changing long-held beliefs, or supporting policies with uncertain outcomes. Without trust, even the most credible expert struggles to persuade anyone to venture beyond their comfort zone.

The Architecture of Credibility: Competence, Reliability, and Dynamism

Credibility operates as a multidimensional construct that audiences continuously assess and reassess throughout persuasive interactions. Communication researchers identify three primary components that together determine perceived credibility: competence, reliability, and dynamism. Competence encompasses the persuader's knowledge, expertise, and intellectual capability within the relevant domain. When epidemiologists model disease transmission patterns during a pandemic, their competence derives from advanced training in statistical modeling, infectious disease mechanisms, and population health dynamics. Audiences evaluate competence through credentials, track records, demonstrated mastery of complex information, and the ability to answer probing questions without evasion or oversimplification. A persuader may possess genuine expertise, but if audiences cannot perceive that competence through observable indicators, it contributes nothing to persuasive effectiveness.

Reliability refers to consistency, dependability, and follow-through on commitments over time. This dimension addresses whether persuaders deliver what they promise, maintain consistent positions rather than opportunistically shifting with circumstances, and prove themselves dependable when the stakes are high. Consider investment advisors: competence alone doesn't establish credibility if advisors consistently fail to return client calls, provide conflicting recommendations based on their mood, or abandon clients during market volatility. Reliability builds through accumulated evidence of steady character and dependable behavior across varied situations. Research on reputation formation demonstrates that people weigh negative reliability evidence approximately four times more heavily than positive instances—a single significant breach of reliability can erase years of consistent performance. This asymmetry means that maintaining credibility requires vigilance; the work of building trust spans years, but credibility can evaporate in moments when reliability falters.

Dynamism captures qualities of energy, enthusiasm, boldness, and charisma that make persuaders compelling beyond their technical competence. Two policy experts may possess identical qualifications and reliability, yet one persuades far more effectively because audiences perceive them as passionate, confident, and inspiring rather than monotonous or tentative. Dynamism explains why certain professors attract packed lecture halls while equally knowledgeable colleagues teach empty seats, or why some corporate leaders inspire organizational transformation while others merely manage existing operations. This dimension operates partly through nonverbal communication—vocal variety, gesture, facial expressiveness—but also through linguistic choices that convey certainty, vision, and forward momentum. Excessive dynamism without corresponding competence and reliability produces the empty charisma of charlatans and demagogues; insufficient dynamism renders even brilliant experts ineffectual at persuading beyond narrow specialist audiences.

The interaction among these three components creates credibility profiles that suit different persuasive contexts. Courtroom expert witnesses maximize competence and reliability while moderating dynamism to project scholarly objectivity; motivational speakers amplify dynamism while establishing sufficient competence and reliability to avoid seeming superficial; investigative journalists balance all three dimensions to maintain audience confidence in both their findings and their interpretative frameworks. Mismatches between credibility profiles and contextual expectations create persuasive friction. A physician who approaches patient consultations with high dynamism and enthusiasm but insufficient displays of reliability—arriving late, interrupting frequently, dismissing patient concerns—undermines persuasive effectiveness despite medical competence. Understanding these components allows persuaders to diagnose credibility deficits and strategically strengthen specific dimensions most relevant to their persuasive objectives.

Trust as Social Contract: The Vulnerability Exchange

Trust fundamentally involves accepting vulnerability based on expectations about another party's future behavior in situations where monitoring or enforcement proves impossible. This vulnerability distinguishes trust from credibility assessment; we might find a used car salesperson credible regarding automotive knowledge while refusing to trust them with purchase negotiations. Philosopher Annette Baier characterized trust as "accepted vulnerability to another's power to harm one, a power inseparable from the power to help." When patients trust physicians with intimate health information, employees trust organizations with career investments, or citizens trust journalists with information filtering, they're entering implicit social contracts in which the trusted party gains power that could be exploited but is expected to be exercised responsibly.

The decision to extend trust involves unconscious risk calculation, weighing potential benefits against the costs of vulnerability. Behavioral economists studying trust games—experimental paradigms where participants decide whether to share resources with partners who could reciprocate or defect—find that trust decisions reflect assessments of four key factors: the other party's perceived benevolence (genuine concern for our welfare), their integrity (adherence to acceptable principles), their predictability (consistency enabling reliable expectations), and the severity of potential betrayal. Someone might trust a colleague with minor workplace responsibilities but not with career-defining projects; the vulnerability threshold shifts based on stakes. This calculus explains why trust develops incrementally through graduated exchanges that test trustworthiness at escalating risk levels. New relationships typically begin with low-stakes trust tests—minor commitments, small disclosures, limited vulnerability—before progressing toward deeper trust as positive experiences accumulate.

Cultural contexts dramatically shape trust norms and expectations. Societies characterized by high institutional trust—where citizens generally expect government agencies, corporations, and professional bodies to operate reliably and ethically—produce different persuasive environments than low-trust cultures where people assume institutional actors pursue self-interest without constraint. Scandinavian countries consistently score highest on generalized social trust measures, meaning citizens extend baseline trust to strangers and institutions; Mediterranean and Latin American countries typically show lower baseline trust, requiring stronger personal relationship foundations before trust develops. These cultural variations profoundly affect persuasion: in high-trust contexts, institutional credentials alone may suffice for initial credibility; in low-trust environments, persuaders must invest substantially in personal relationship building before audiences will seriously consider their messages. Neither approach is inherently superior; they represent different adaptations to varying historical experiences with institutional reliability.

Digital communication technologies have introduced novel trust challenges that previous generations never confronted. Online interactions often lack the embodied cues—facial expressions, vocal tone, physical presence—those humans evolved to assess when evaluating trustworthiness. Social media enables identity deception at scales previously impossible; fake profiles, deepfake videos, and coordinated bot networks can manufacture credibility signals while concealing actual sources. Research on online trust formation reveals that people substitute alternative trust indicators in digital contexts: user reviews and ratings, social proof through follower counts, platform verification badges, and digital reputation systems. These proxies imperfectly substitute for direct trustworthiness assessment, creating opportunities for sophisticated manipulation. A persuader might accumulate thousands of purchased followers to signal popularity, fake positive reviews to suggest reliability, or use search engine optimization to appear authoritative. The persuasion landscape increasingly requires audiences to navigate between genuine credibility and manufactured simulacra, while persuaders must recognize that audiences approach digital claims with heightened skepticism.

The Trust Reservoir: Accumulation and Depletion Dynamics

Trust functions as a reservoir that accumulates gradually through consistent positive interactions but can drain rapidly through betrayals or inconsistencies. This asymmetry—trust builds slowly, erodes quickly—reflects evolutionary psychology shaped by ancestral environments where misplaced trust in dangerous individuals or groups carried severe survival consequences. Psychological research on negativity bias demonstrates that humans weigh negative information approximately two to three times more heavily than equivalent positive information when forming judgments. For trust specifically, the bias intensifies: studies of organizational trust show that trust-violating incidents require roughly five trust-building interactions to neutralize their impact. A manager who cancels a promised promotion erases months of trust-building through reliable delegation and honest feedback. This mathematical reality means persuaders cannot treat trust maintenance casually; the investment required to restore depleted trust vastly exceeds the effort needed to maintain existing trust reservoirs.

Understanding trust dynamics transforms how effective persuaders approach their communication strategies over time. Rather than viewing each persuasive encounter as isolated, sophisticated influence agents recognize that every interaction either deposits into or withdraws from long-term trust accounts. A financial advisor who recommends a particular investment implicitly promises future performance; if that investment succeeds, trust increases, and subsequent recommendations receive more favorable consideration. If it fails, trust depletes not merely in proportion to financial losses but is amplified by the violation of implicit promises. Strategic persuaders, therefore, become selective about commitments, making only promises they can reliably fulfill and clearly communicating uncertainty when outcomes remain genuinely unpredictable. The counterintuitive insight is that sometimes refusing to persuade—declining to make claims one cannot adequately support—constitutes the most effective long-term persuasion strategy by preserving trust reservoirs for situations where confidence is justified.

Organizations that institutionalize trust-building practices gain persuasive advantages that competitors cannot easily replicate. The Ritz-Carlton hotel chain empowers every employee to spend up to $2,000 resolving guest problems without management approval policy that seems financially reckless until recognized as a strategic trust investment. When a housekeeper notices a guest has forgotten prescription medication and arranges emergency pharmacy delivery, or a concierge personally drives to retrieve a laptop left in a taxi, these extraordinary responses create trust reservoirs that transcend typical hospitality service. Guests develop confidence that the organization genuinely prioritizes their well-being over immediate costs, making them receptive to premium pricing, loyalty program enrollment, and positive word of mouth, which serves as third-party persuasion. The two-thousand-dollar discretionary budget paradoxically costs less than it generates, as it converts satisfied customers into committed advocates whose testimonials carry credibility that paid advertising cannot buy.

The trust reservoir model also explains why specific organizations survive scandals that would destroy others with shallow trust foundations. When Toyota faced massive recalls in 2009-2010 for unintended acceleration problems affecting millions of vehicles, their previously accumulated trust reservoir cushioned the crisis impact—decades of reliability had established deep trust among consumers who interpreted the crisis as an aberration rather than a revelation of fundamental untrustworthiness. Toyota's transparent response—publicly accepting responsibility, implementing comprehensive fixes, and communicating openly throughout the process—further drew upon and ultimately reinforced that trust foundation. Contrast this with companies entering crises with depleted trust reservoirs: Volkswagen's emissions scandal proved devastating, partly because prior corporate behavior had already eroded public trust in its environmental claims. The same crisis magnitude produces radically different outcomes depending on pre-existing trust reservoirs, demonstrating that credibility and trust function as insurance policies that prove most valuable during reputation storms.

Repairing Damaged Credibility: The Reconstruction Process

When credibility suffers damage—through broken commitments, exposed incompetence, or ethical violations, reconstruction requires strategic sequences that most persuaders instinctively handle poorly. Natural impulse involves immediate justification, deflecting blame, or minimizing the significance of the breach. Research on effective apologies and trust repair reveals these intuitive responses typically deepen damage rather than initiate healing. Audiences interpreting these defensive responses conclude that the persuader cares more about protecting reputation than acknowledging harm, further eroding already damaged credibility. Effective reconstruction follows a counterintuitive sequence that begins with unconditional acknowledgment of the specific violation without immediate excuses or contextualization.

The acknowledgment phase requires explicitly naming the specific trust breach and taking clear ownership, without hedging language. Compare "mistakes were made" versus "I provided inaccurate cost projections that led your team to approve an underfunded initiative, and I take full responsibility for that analytical failure." The passive construction in the first statement obscures agency; the second statement demonstrates the precision of acknowledgment that audiences require before considering credibility restoration. This precision signals that the persuader understands exactly what occurred and accepts accountability, addressing the fear that someone who doesn't fully grasp their violation might repeat it. Neurological research using fMRI during apology processing shows that the brain responds differently to specific acknowledgments than to vague admissions—precise language activates trust-associated neural regions, while ambiguous apologies maintain threat-response activation.

Following acknowledgment, effective trust repair requires articulating a genuine understanding of harm caused from the affected party's perspective. This empathetic recognition addresses a fundamental question audiences ask when deciding whether to restore trust: Does this person actually comprehend what their actions cost us, or do they merely regret getting caught? A technology company CEO addressing a data breach might say: "I understand this violation means many of you now face identity theft risks, spend hours changing passwords and monitoring credit reports, and experience ongoing anxiety about financial security. This isn't merely a technical failure; it's a disruption to your peace of mind and daily life." This phase transforms abstract violations into recognized human consequences, demonstrating that the persuader grasps impacts beyond their own reputation damage.

The reconstruction sequence then requires explaining what systemic changes will prevent recurrence without positioning these reforms as excuses for the original violation. This distinction proves subtle but critical:

audiences need confidence that trust-violating circumstances won't repeat, but premature explanations of mitigating factors read as justification rather than prevention. Only after clearly acknowledging the violation and recognizing its harm can persuaders productively discuss procedural changes, additional safeguards, or structural reforms that address root causes. A physician whose diagnostic error harmed a patient might explain: "I've now implemented a mandatory second-opinion protocol for diagnoses of this complexity and scheduled additional training in the relevant diagnostic techniques. These changes don't excuse my error, but they reflect my commitment to ensuring it never happens again." The sequencing communicates that reforms arise from genuine learning rather than reputation management.

Finally, credibility reconstruction requires sustained behavioral consistency over extended timeframes that demonstrate claimed reforms represent genuine transformation rather than temporary performance. Trust researchers identify this as the "cheap talk" problem— promises about future behavior cost nothing to make but everything to keep. Audiences have learned through experience that people frequently promise change during crises but revert to problematic patterns once immediate pressure subsides. Sustained consistency over six months to two years provides the behavioral evidence that persuaders have internalized reforms rather than merely performed contrition. During this reconstruction phase, effective persuaders recognize they occupy a probationary status in which audiences scrutinize their actions more intensively than before the trust violation. Rather than resenting this heightened scrutiny, strategic persuaders embrace it as information that allows audiences to verify trustworthiness through direct observation rather than blind faith. The willingness to accept earned distrust paradoxically accelerates trust restoration by demonstrating the humility and self-awareness that genuine trustworthiness requires.

Credibility Transfer and Third-Party Validation

One of the most potent yet underutilized persuasion strategies involve credibility transfer through third-party validation. When persuaders face credibility deficits—perhaps because they're unknown to audiences, represent groups facing skepticism, or advocate positions that trigger defensive resistance—borrowing credibility from trusted intermediaries can bypass barriers that direct persuasion cannot penetrate. This principle explains why pharmaceutical companies fund research at independent universities rather than relying solely on internal studies; why social movements recruit celebrity spokespersons despite their lack of relevant expertise; and why startups desperately seek venture capital from prestigious firms whose endorsement matters more than their funding.

Credibility transfer operates through association principles deeply embedded in human cognition. When an audience trusts Person A and Person A explicitly endorses Person B, the audience automatically extends provisional trust to Person B, even without direct evidence of their trustworthiness. This cognitive shortcut evolved as an efficient way to expand trust networks beyond personal experience. In ancestral environments, knowing that your trusted friend vouches for a stranger provided valuable information about whether that stranger warranted cooperation. Modern persuasion contexts exploit this mechanism constantly: political candidates compete for newspaper editorial endorsements, authors seek foreword contributions from established figures in their fields, and job seekers leverage LinkedIn recommendations from respected colleagues. The transfer isn't completed. Individuals must eventually demonstrate direct credibility—but it grants access and initial receptivity that they might never achieve through self-promotion alone.

The effectiveness of credibility transfer depends critically on alignment between the validator's credibility domain and the persuasion context. A Nobel Prize-winning physicist lending credibility to climate science communication effectively transfers relevant expertise; that same physicist endorsing dietary supplements trades on prestige in an unrelated domain, potentially damaging both their credibility and the transfer attempt. Audiences intuitively assess transfer appropriateness: we accept film directors recommending cinematographers but question their automotive engineering opinions. Strategic persuaders, therefore, seek validators whose credibility domains align closely with persuasion objectives and whose audiences overlap substantially with target populations. A healthcare startup targeting rural elderly populations gains more from an endorsement by a trusted rural family physician than from a Silicon Valley tech celebrity, even though the latter has higher general prestige.

Third-party validation proves especially potent when validators possess credibility that persuaders inherently cannot claim. Scientific researchers establishing new findings face the challenge of arguing for claims that aren't yet accepted as truth; peer review serves as a mechanism for credibility transfer, where established experts validate novel contributions. Similarly, reformed extremists advocating deradicalization possess credibility with active extremists that entirely lack—their lived experience and insider knowledge create trust that no amount of academic credentials could generate. This principle suggests that effective persuasion campaigns deliberately recruit diverse

validators whose varied credibility sources collectively
address audience skepticism from multiple angles. A climate
action campaign might deploy atmospheric scientists for
technical credibility, economists for financial viability
assessments, religious leaders for moral framing, and
military officials for national security implications. This
credibility coalition recognizes that audiences are
heterogeneous; validators who persuade one audience
segment might alienate another, requiring strategic diversity
in endorsement portfolios.

The digital age has democratized the transfer of credibility
through mechanisms such as online reviews, influencer
marketing, and crowdsourced recommendations. These
distributed validation systems aggregate credibility signals
from numerous low-credibility sources into collectively
persuasive endorsements. A restaurant with 504 five-star
reviews persuades more effectively than one whose owners
claim excellence; crowdsourced validation conveys
credibility that self-promotion cannot. However, digital
credibility transfer systems are vulnerable to exploitation
through fake reviews, purchased testimonials, and
coordinated manipulation campaigns. Sophisticated
audiences increasingly recognize these vulnerabilities,
requiring persuaders to ensure third-party validations
maintain genuine independence. The most credible
validation occurs when validators incur costs, whether
reputational risks by endorsing controversial positions,
financial investment in products they recommend, or time
expenditure providing detailed assessments. Costly signals
are more complex to fake, carrying a proportionally greater
potential for credibility transfer than effortless
endorsements that commitment-free digital contexts enable.

When implementing credibility transfer strategies,
persuaders must navigate the authenticity paradox:

audiences need to perceive endorsements as genuine rather than purchased, yet persuaders typically must actively recruit and compensate validators. Transparent disclosure of material relationships" this review reflects a product I received free for evaluation purposes"—preserves authenticity while acknowledging commercial arrangements. Research on disclosure effectiveness reveals that audiences accept compensated endorsements as legitimate when validators maintain editorial independence and the relationship is clearly communicated. What destroys credibility transfer is the discovered hidden relationships: influencers promoting products without disclosing sponsorships, or academic researchers publishing industry-funded studies without acknowledging financial ties. The appearance of concealed incentives suggests persuaders recognize their case couldn't withstand scrutiny if audiences understood the endorsement's true nature, triggering suspicion that extends beyond the specific instance to contaminate the persuader's entire credibility reservoir. Strategic credibility transfer, therefore, requires transparency that may seem to undermine persuasive effectiveness but strengthens long-term trust by demonstrating respect for audience autonomy.

The most sophisticated approach to credibility and trust in persuasion recognizes that these aren't merely communication tactics but fundamental commitments that shape every aspect of how influence occurs. Persuaders who treat credibility as something to strategically perform rather than authentically embody inevitably face discovery as audiences detect inconsistencies between projected and actual trustworthiness. The Johnson & Johnson example that opened this chapter illustrates the profound insight that sometimes the most persuasive action involves decisions that superficially seem unrelated to persuasion—product recalls, process transparency, or admissions of uncertainty.

These moves work precisely because they demonstrate that the persuader prioritizes genuine trustworthiness over immediate persuasive success, the very commitment that makes sustained influence possible. In the final analysis, credibility and trust aren't tools that persuaders employ; their foundations that determine whether persuasion attempts will even register as worthy of audience consideration or be dismissed as manipulation from sources unworthy of serious engagement.

Chapter 6: Social Proof and Group Dynamics

When seventeen-year-old Charlie Allnut stood outside a London nightclub in 2019, he faced a decision that would cost him his life. The venue had reached capacity, yet hundreds of young people continued surging forward, crushing those at the front against metal barriers. Security footage later revealed that Charlie repeatedly looked around, observing others pushing forward, and, despite visible distress, he continued pressing ahead rather than retreating. His final movements showed him glancing sideways at peers who were also making a gesture recognized by crowd dynamics researchers as "social referencing" the instinctive human tendency to calibrate behavior by observing those around us. Charlie's tragic death in that crowd crush illustrates the darkest potential of social proof: our evolved tendency to look to others for behavioral guidance can override even basic survival instincts when group signals contradict personal perception.

This phenomenon extends far beyond emergencies into virtually every domain where humans make decisions. Social proof operates as a fundamental heuristic through which individuals determine appropriate behavior by observing others' behavior, particularly in conditions of uncertainty or ambiguity. The mechanism evolved because our ancestors who successfully learned from observing group behaviors which foods were safe, which paths led to water, which strangers might prove dangerous—survived at higher rates than those who ignored social information. Modern humans inherit a neural architecture optimized for social learning, with specialized brain regions, including the posterior superior temporal sulcus and temporoparietal junction, that activate specifically when processing information about others' actions and intentions. Understanding social proof and group dynamics reveals persuasion operating not through individual cognitive processes but through collective behavioral patterns that shape individual choices, often without conscious awareness.

The persuasive power of social proof is most evident when individuals have incomplete information and must rely on external cues to navigate uncertainty. Neuroimaging studies conducted by Vasily Klucharev at the Donders Institute demonstrate that when experimental subjects observe their opinions diverging from group consensus, their brains show activation in the rostral cingulate zone—the same region associated with error detection and conflict monitoring. The brain literally processes disagreement with group consensus as a type of mistake requiring correction. This neurological response occurs automatically, before conscious deliberation, explaining why social proof influences behavior even when individuals claim independence from others' opinions. The persuasive force of social proof bypasses rational evaluation by triggering ancient neural circuitry that equates group consensus with correctness.

The Plurality Effect: When Numbers Override Evidence

Social proof operates along a continuum in which persuasive impact intensifies as the number of people demonstrating behavior increases. However, the relationship follows a logarithmic rather than a linear pattern. Research conducted by behavioral economist Dan Ariely, examining online product reviews, discovered that a product with five positive reviews generated substantially more purchases than one with no reviews, but increasing from fifty to one hundred positive reviews produced minimal additional impact. This diminishing-returns pattern reflects how the human brain processes quantity information: the difference between zero social proof and some social proof produces dramatic psychological shifts, while adding to already substantial social proof yields only marginal additional persuasion. The implication for persuaders proves counterintuitive— achieving modest initial social proof often matters more strategically than accumulating overwhelming numbers.

The plurality effect also demonstrates the influence of moderating factors, including group composition and observer similarity. Solomon Asch's conformity experiments in the 1950s established that individuals would deny clear perceptual evidence—claiming two obviously different lines were identical—when confederates unanimously provided incorrect answers. However, subsequent research by Allen and Levine revealed that conformity pressure diminished dramatically when even one confederate broke from group consensus, regardless of that dissenter's apparent competence. A single person agreeing with the subject's accurate perception reduced conformity from 32% to just 5.5%, demonstrating that unanimity matters more than absolute numbers for social proof effects. This finding explains why dissent proves so threatening to organizations that rely on social proof for compliance: one visible objector can shatter the conformity pressure that required dozens of conforming voices to establish.

Contemporary digital environments amplify social proof effects while simultaneously creating opportunities for manipulation that previous generations never confronted. Restaurant review platforms, social media engagement metrics, and e-commerce rating systems transform formerly private consumption decisions into public displays of social proof. When prospective diners see that 847 previous customers rated a restaurant 4.7 stars, they're receiving synthesized social proof from hundreds of strangers whose individual judgments they'll never evaluate. Platform designers recognize social proof's persuasive power and architect choice environments to maximize its impact: Airbnb displays "Booked 6 times in the last 24 hours" messages; Booking.com warns "Only two rooms left at this price"; Amazon highlights products as "Amazon's Choice" with notification badges. These interventions don't merely report social proof—they actively construct it, selecting which metrics to display, how to visualize quantity, and when to introduce scarcity cues that trigger urgency.

The digital manipulation of social proof reaches concerning sophistication in phenomena like astroturfing—the practice of manufacturing grassroots social proof through fake reviews, purchased followers, or coordinated inauthentic behavior. Research by Filippo Menczer at Indiana University analyzing social media manipulation found that approximately 9-15% of active Twitter accounts during the 2016 U.S. presidential election were bots designed to create artificial social proof by amplifying specific messages, making fringe positions appear mainstream. The bots did not change individual minds through argumentation but generated the appearance of consensus, triggering social proof mechanisms that shift perceptions of what views are normal or acceptable. This manufactured social proof is hard to detect because it exploits the exact psychological mechanisms as authentic social proof, making it increasingly difficult for audiences to distinguish genuine consensus from an orchestrated appearance of agreement.

Informational vs. Normative Social Influence: Two Pathways to Conformity

Social proof operates through two distinct psychological mechanisms that produce behavioral conformity through different underlying processes. Informational social influence occurs when individuals genuinely change their private beliefs or attitudes because they interpret others' behavior as providing valid information about objective reality. When drivers slow down upon seeing other vehicles stopped ahead, they're engaging in informational social influence—inferring from others' behavior that potential hazards exist even before personally perceiving the obstruction. This type of influence produces internalized attitude change rather than mere public compliance. Research by Muzafer Sherif using the autokinetic effect—an optical illusion where a stationary light appears to move in darkness—demonstrated that when individuals made judgments in groups, their estimates converged toward group norms and remained stable even when later tested alone. The group consensus had fundamentally changed their private perception of reality.

Normative social influence, by contrast, produces compliance without necessarily changing private attitudes. This mechanism operates through desire for social acceptance, fear of rejection, or pursuit of rewards contingent on conformity. Teenagers who begin smoking despite knowing health risks often exemplify normative social influence— they're conforming to gain peer acceptance rather than genuinely revising their beliefs about smoking's dangers. The compliance remains contingent on social monitoring; behavior reverts when observation ceases. Deutsch and Gerard's experimental studies, which separated these two influence types, found that normative influence dominated when responses were public and individuals could be identified, while informational influence prevailed when responses were anonymous. The task involved objective judgments, for which the group might possess superior knowledge.

Understanding this distinction transforms persuasion strategy because the two mechanisms require different interventions and produce different stability over time. Persuaders seeking lasting behavioral change must target informational social influence by positioning the desired behavior as providing valid information about reality, not merely demonstrating which actions gain approval. Anti-smoking campaigns that shifted from emphasizing peer disapproval to revealing tobacco industry manipulation succeeded partly by converting smoking into an informational question—"What does smoking signal about your independence?"—rather than purely normative conformity pressure. When individuals perceive they're learning truth from social proof rather than just conforming for acceptance, the resulting attitude change persists across contexts and resists counter-persuasion more effectively.

The relationship between informational and normative influence becomes more complex in ambiguous situations, where both mechanisms operate simultaneously. Consider investment behavior during market bubbles: investors observing others purchasing rapidly appreciating assets face both informational questions ("Do they know something about fundamental value that I'm missing?") and normative pressures ("Will I appear foolish to colleagues if I fail to participate in obvious gains?"). Behavioral economist Robert Shiller's research on speculative bubbles reveals that these dual mechanisms create cascades where initial price increases generate social proof that attracts additional investors, whose participation validates the original investors' judgment, creating self-reinforcing cycles that disconnect asset prices from fundamental values. The persuasive power of social proof becomes circular—behavior itself generates the social information that justifies further behavior, requiring no external validation until bubble dynamics reverse catastrophically.

Reference Group Selection: The Hidden Architecture of Social Proof

Social proof's persuasive impact depends critically on which reference groups individuals consult when seeking behavioral guidance, yet people rarely consciously select reference groups through deliberate analysis. Instead, reference group selection follows largely automatic processes influenced by contextual cues, identity considerations, and perceived similarity. Research by sociologist Robert Merton, distinguishing between membership groups (those we actually belong to) and reference groups (those we use for behavioral standards), revealed that people often orient behavior toward groups they aspire to join rather than groups they currently inhabit. Medical students adopt professional mannerisms of attending physicians years before achieving that status; teenagers emulate celebrities whose lifestyles they'll never directly experience. This aspirational reference group orientation creates persuasion opportunities for those who can position behaviors as characteristic of admired groups.

The matching principle demonstrates that social proof's persuasive power increases dramatically when the demonstrating group shares relevant characteristics with the target audience. Health psychologists studying organ donation registration discovered that campaign messages featuring demographically similar donors—matching age, ethnicity, and gender—produced significantly higher registration rates than messages featuring dissimilar donors or generic appeals. The effect persisted even when objective similarity was superficial: college students shown social proof that "students at your university" supported organ donation registered at higher rates than those shown identical numbers of donors from other universities. This finding reveals that social proof operates through perceived similarity rather than absolute quantity, suggesting that niche influence from relevant subgroups often outperforms mass influence from undifferentiated crowds.

Strategic reference group framing allows persuaders to activate particular group identities and corresponding behavioral norms even when multiple potential reference groups exist. Environmental psychologists working with hotel guests found that towel-reuse messages emphasizing "Guests who stayed in this room" led to higher towel-reuse rates (49.3%) than messages emphasizing "Guests in this hotel" (44.1%) or generic environmental appeals (37.2%). The hyperlocal reference group—previous occupants of the same room—exerted more substantial normative influence than broader categories, despite representing fewer people overall. This paradox illustrates that psychological proximity matters more than numerical majority: people weigh social proof from psychologically near reference groups far more heavily than abstract majorities. The persuasion insight involves identifying which reference group frame produces the strongest identification, rather than which represents the largest number.

Professional persuaders increasingly employ sophisticated reference-group targeting through digital microtargeting capabilities that previous communicators never had. Political campaigns using psychographic profiling can present different social proof to different audience segments based on likely reference group orientation: showing younger voters that "millennials in your neighborhood support this candidate," while showing older voters that "retirees like you choose this policy." This granular reference-group tailoring operates invisibly—different audiences receive different social proof cues designed to activate their particular reference-group identities, all while maintaining the appearance of objective reporting on popularity. The ethical implications remain contested: does this represent sophisticated matching of social proof to relevant reference groups, or manipulative presentation of selective social proof that conceals actual diversity of opinion?

Pluralistic Ignorance and the Spiral of Silence

One of social proof's most fascinating paradoxes concerns situations in which private attitudes diverge dramatically from public behavior. Yet individuals misperceive group consensus, observing others' public conformity while remaining unaware of their private dissent. Pluralistic ignorance describes conditions where most group members privately reject a norm but mistakenly believe others accept it, leading each individual to continue public conformity to avoid appearing deviant. Research by Deborah Prentice and Dale Miller examining college student drinking attitudes found that most students felt personally uncomfortable with campus alcohol consumption levels but estimated that peers felt more comfortable, leading individuals to consume more alcohol than they privately preferred to conform to misperceived norms. The collective result: campus drinking culture that nobody privately endorses but everyone publicly reinforces, creating genuine social proof for attitudes nobody actually holds.

This phenomenon explains the persistence of numerous social practices that participants privately question but collectively perpetuate. Corporate cultures featuring excessive work hours, political environments where dissent appears absent, or social groups where individuals engage in activities they privately dislike may all reflect pluralistic ignorance rather than genuine consensus. The persuasive implications are profound: apparent social proof may reflect coordination on public behavior rather than authentic collective preference. Breaking pluralistic ignorance requires public disclosure of private attitudes, allowing individuals to recognize that others share their doubts. Social psychologist Mahzarin Banaji's experiments demonstrated that when researchers revealed private attitude distributions to participants who had misperceived group consensus, behavioral conformity reduced dramatically as individuals recognized their private views represented the silent majority rather than deviant minority positions.

The spiral of silence theory, developed by political scientist Elisabeth Noelle-Neumann, describes a related dynamic where individuals who perceive their opinions as minority positions become reluctant to express them publicly, fearing social isolation. This reluctance creates a self-fulfilling prophecy: as holders of one position remain silent while others speak, the vocal position gains disproportionate visibility, further reinforcing the perception that it represents the majority, which in turn leads to additional silence from those holding contrary views. The spiral accelerates until one position dominates public discourse despite potentially representing only a slight actual majority or even a vocal minority whose willingness to speak creates false social proof of numerical dominance. Contemporary research by communication scholars examining social media discourse finds that the spiral of silence effects may amplify online, where visible engagement metrics (likes, shares, retweets) create explicit social proof that influences which opinions individuals feel safe expressing.

Persuaders can strategically exploit pluralistic ignorance and the spiral of silence dynamics, though doing so raises significant ethical concerns. Astroturfing campaigns that create an artificial appearance of grassroots support may trigger a spiral effect in which individuals with genuine grassroots opposition remain silent, believing themselves isolated when they actually represent substantial constituencies. Conversely, ethical persuaders working to change harmful social norms—such as bullying, discrimination, and environmental damage—may intentionally break pluralistic ignorance by publicizing that private attitudes already oppose the behavior, thereby undermining the false social proof that sustains the practice. Montana's "Most of Us" campaign, addressing college binge drinking, successfully reduced alcohol consumption by revealing actual student attitudes: survey data showed most students drank moderately and felt uncomfortable with heavy drinking culture, contrary to pluralistic ignorance that had sustained excessive drinking through false social proof. Making private attitudes visible transformed perceived norms, allowing majority preferences to generate social proof aligned with actual rather than misperceived consensus.

Deindividuation and Emergent Group Behavior

When individuals merge into crowds, fundamental psychological shifts occur that transform decision-making processes and create collective behavioral patterns irreducible to individual psychology. Deindividuation theory, originating with Leon Festinger and later developed by Philip Zimbardo, describes psychological states characterized by reduced self-awareness, weakened self-regulation, and increased responsiveness to immediate situational cues that emerge when people perceive themselves as anonymous group members rather than identifiable individuals.

Research examining crowd behavior during protests, concerts, and riots reveals that deindividuated individuals engage in actions—both prosocial and antisocial—that they would reject under conditions of individual accountability. The phenomenon occurs not through a deliberate choice to abandon personal standards, but through psychological submersion in collective identity, in which group-level norms temporarily override individual moral frameworks.

The Stanford Prison Experiment, despite its controversial methodology, illuminated aspects of deindividuation's psychological mechanisms. Guards who adopted roles in the simulated prison environment exhibited increasingly aggressive behavior partly because uniforms, mirrored sunglasses, and collective guard identity reduced individual self-awareness while heightening identification with group role. The deindividuation didn't eliminate moral reasoning—participants later expressed genuine shock at their behavior—but temporarily subordinated individual moral frameworks to situational demands and perceived group expectations. More rigorous subsequent research by Stephen Reicher, examining actual crowd events, found that deindividuated crowds don't descend into chaos but rather follow alternative normative structures defined by emergent group identity. Soccer hooligans operating as deindividuated crowd members follow sophisticated tactical coordination and internal group norms, demonstrating that deindividuation produces not normlessness but substitution of group norms for individual standards.

Contemporary digital environments create novel forms of deindividuation through online anonymity and psychological distance that separates communicators from the consequences of their messages. Research examining online harassment and disinhibition effects demonstrates that people express views and engage in behaviors they would inhibit in face-to-face contexts when communicating through anonymous or pseudonymous digital identities. The persuasive implications extend beyond individual behavior change to collective phenomena such as viral social proof cascades, in which individuals share content without careful evaluation because they perceive themselves as part of a collective movement rather than as individually accountable sharers. The Ice Bucket Challenge's viral spread demonstrated how deindividuation, in a positive sense, could mobilize collective action: participants perceived themselves as joining a larger social movement, thereby reducing individual self-consciousness about posting videos of themselves performing unusual behavior.

Persuaders working in group contexts must recognize that collective psychology operates according to principles different from those of individual persuasion. Interventions effective with individuals—emphasizing personal responsibility, highlighting uniqueness, encouraging independent decision-making—may prove counterproductive in group contexts where deindividuation already operates. Instead, effective collective persuasion works with rather than against deindividuation dynamics by establishing desired group norms, creating appropriate collective identities, and channeling rather than suppressing the psychological energy of merged group consciousness. Civil rights movement organizers recognized this principle when crafting nonviolent protest strategies: rather than relying solely on individual moral conviction, they created powerful collective identities (freedom riders, lunch counter protesters) with explicit behavioral norms that channeled deindividuated energy into disciplined nonviolent action. The persuasive architecture worked through group psychology rather than individual cognition, recognizing that merged collective consciousness could be directed but not eliminated.

Social Contagion: Ideas as Infectious Agents

Behaviors, emotions, and beliefs spread through social networks following patterns remarkably similar to those of infectious disease transmission, suggesting that social influence operates through contagion mechanisms in which exposure to demonstrators increases the likelihood that observers adopt the behavior. Network science research analyzing social contagion reveals that the probability of behavioral adoption depends on three factors: transmission rate (the possibility that exposure leads to adoption), network structure (the number of potential exposures each person receives), and adoption threshold (the number of exposures required before adoption occurs). Simple behaviors with low adoption thresholds—using new slang terms, trying trending restaurants, adopting fashion trends—spread rapidly because single exposure often suffices for transmission. Complex behaviors requiring skill development, resource investment, or norm violation spread more slowly because multiple exposures are necessary before individuals cross adoption thresholds.

Sociologist Duncan Watts' experiments with artificial cultural markets demonstrated that social contagion could create hit songs and bestselling products essentially randomly through collective behavioral cascades. Researchers created parallel digital markets in which participants downloaded songs while observing different social proofs about what others had downloaded. The same songs became hits or failures across different markets depending on initial random variation in downloads, demonstrating that quality alone didn't determine success—social contagion amplified small initial advantages into massive popularity differences. Crucially, the most popular songs across markets varied dramatically despite identical available choices, revealing that social proof creates unpredictable winner-take-all dynamics in which early adopters' preferences determine outcomes through cascading influence. This finding challenges the assumption that popularity reliably reflects quality; instead, quality establishes a minimum threshold, while social contagion determines the distribution of success above that floor.

Emotional contagion represents a potent form of social influence operating through largely automatic processes that bypass conscious evaluation. Neurological research using facial electromyography demonstrates that when people observe others expressing emotions, their own facial muscles activate mimicking those expressions within milliseconds— too rapidly for conscious processing. This automatic mimicry feeds back into emotional experience through facial feedback mechanisms, leading observers to experience emotions they've mimicked. The result: emotions spread through groups at neurological speed, creating collective emotional states that emerge from interpersonal synchronization rather than shared objective circumstances. Traders on stock exchange floors experience collective anxiety or euphoria through emotional contagion; stadium crowds synchronize excitement; digital mobs coordinate outrage through distributed emotional convergence.

Strategic persuaders increasingly recognize social contagion's power and attempt to engineer viral spread through "seeding" strategies that identify optimal initial adopters whose network positions enable widespread transmission. Marketing researchers analyzing successful viral campaigns found that influencer marketing succeeds not primarily through reach (the number of followers an influencer has) but through the activation of network structures that enable cascade dynamics. A product endorsed by an influencer whose followers are themselves well-connected and prone to sharing creates multi-level transmission chains. Conversely, influencers whose followers remain relatively isolated from broader networks may generate initial visibility without producing cascading adoption. The persuasion insight is that social proof doesn't merely demonstrate popularity—it can actively create popularity through contagion dynamics that transform early adopters into transmission vectors whose influence propagates through network structures invisible primarily to both persuaders and adopters.

Human beings evolved as fundamentally social creatures whose survival depended on successful integration into cooperative groups. This evolutionary heritage means persuasion never operates purely at the individual level—social context, group dynamics, reference group identities, and collective behavioral norms shape every persuasive encounter. Understanding social proof and group dynamics reveals that changing behavior often requires changing social environments rather than changing individual minds. The most powerful persuasive interventions don't convince isolated individuals through superior arguments but transform social proof signals, shift reference group norms, activate collective identities, or harness contagion dynamics that make new behaviors appear normal, desirable, and widespread. This collective dimension of persuasion presents both extraordinary opportunities and serious ethical responsibilities for those who recognize that shaping social proof means shaping the behavioral architecture through which millions of individuals make decisions they believe are entirely their own.

Chapter 7: Harnessing the Subconscious: Subliminal Techniques

The human mind processes approximately 11 million pieces of information per second, yet only 40 to 50 bits reach conscious awareness. This staggering disparity reveals a fundamental reality about human cognition: the vast majority of mental processing occurs beneath the threshold of conscious perception, in neural networks that evaluate, categorize, and respond to environmental stimuli without ever troubling our awareness. A sales associate approaches you wearing a subtle citrus fragrance that activates childhood memories of summer vacations; background music in a wine store plays French accordion melodies that mysteriously increase French wine purchases by seventy-six percent; a website loads slightly slower than competitors, triggering unconscious frustration that translates into a fourteen percent decrease in conversion rates. None of these influences announces itself to consciousness, yet each shapes decisions with remarkable precision. Understanding how persuasion operates through these subconscious channels transforms influence from a conscious argument-making enterprise into something far more comprehensive: the strategic architecture of environments, experiences, and stimuli that shape behavior before conscious deliberation begins.

The distinction between subliminal perception and subconscious processing is critical for understanding how modern persuasion ethically and effectively harnesses these mechanisms. Subliminal perception refers specifically to stimuli presented below the threshold of conscious detection—images flashed for milliseconds, sounds played below audible volumes, or messages embedded so subtly that awareness never registers their presence. Subconscious processing, by contrast, encompasses the broader phenomenon of mental activity occurring outside conscious attention, including information that could be consciously perceived but isn't because attention focuses elsewhere. When you drive a familiar route while absorbed in conversation, your subconscious navigation successfully handles complex spatial judgments, traffic pattern assessments, and motor coordination without conscious involvement. This distinction matters because, while truly subliminal persuasion faces both ethical concerns and practical limitations in effectiveness, subconscious persuasion through carefully designed experiences operates constantly and powerfully across domains from retail environments to digital interfaces to political campaigns. The most sophisticated persuaders recognize that conscious argumentation represents merely the visible tip of an influence iceberg whose massive bulk operates entirely beneath the surface of awareness.

The Architecture of Unconscious Influence

Environmental design constitutes perhaps the most pervasive form of subconscious persuasion, silently shaping behavior through spatial arrangements, sensory atmospheres, and contextual cues that bypass analytical evaluation. Consider how casino designers employ what industry insiders call "labyrinth architecture"—deliberately confusing floor plans without clear sight lines to exits, absent windows and clocks to obscure the passage of time, and maze-like pathways that ensure gamblers repeatedly encounter slot machines as they attempt to navigate toward restaurants or restrooms. Researchers studying these environments document that gamblers in windowless casinos with obscured time indicators spend an average of 43 minutes longer per visit than in facilities with natural light and visible clocks. Nobody consciously decides to gamble longer because they cannot see sunlight; instead, the absence of temporal cues prevents the unconscious mechanisms that typically signal "you've been here too long" from activating. The environment persuades by removing information rather than adding arguments.

Retail environments similarly exploit subconscious processing by strategically manipulating ambient factors that influence purchasing behavior, without customers recognizing the mechanisms at work. Supermarkets position produce departments at store entrances specifically because the vibrant colors, fresh scents, and associations with health and vitality create positive affective states that unconsciously transfer to subsequent purchasing decisions throughout the store. Behavioral economists measuring this "fresh start effect" find that shoppers who enter through the produce section spend approximately 23% more on indulgent or unnecessary items in other store areas than customers who enter through different departments. The mechanism operates entirely outside conscious awareness: the positive feelings generated by beautiful produce don't announce themselves as "I feel good because of those tomatoes, therefore I should buy expensive cheese," yet the causal chain operates reliably. Persuasion happens not through what shoppers think, but through what they feel without thinking about why.

Temperature represents another subconscious influence vector that sophisticated persuaders manipulate with surgical precision. Research conducted across multiple retail contexts reveals that slightly cooler temperatures— approximately sixty-seven to sixty-nine degrees Fahrenheit—increase browsing time and purchase likelihood for clothing retailers. In comparison, restaurants optimize revenue by maintaining temperatures between 71 and 73 degrees, which encourages longer dining durations and additional course orders. The thermoregulation occurring unconsciously influences behavioral decisions: cooler temperatures in clothing stores prompt subconscious assessments that trying on warmer garments would feel pleasant. In contrast, optimal restaurant temperatures create physical comfort that extends meal duration without patrons consciously attributing their lingering to ambient temperature. Hotels targeting business travelers maintain lobby temperatures at 68 degrees—cool enough that the warmth of guest rooms feels exceptionally welcoming, unconsciously reinforcing positive associations with the property. These temperature manipulations cost minimal resources while producing measurable behavioral changes, exemplifying how environmental factors persuade through physiological mechanisms that never reach conscious evaluation.

Temporal Manipulation and Decision Architecture

The timing and sequencing of persuasive appeals dramatically influence effectiveness through mechanisms that operate primarily outside conscious awareness. Psychologists studying what they term "temporal framing effects" have discovered that identical proposals generate drastically different acceptance rates depending on when they're presented within daily, weekly, or yearly cycles. Requests for charitable donations increase by thirty-one percent when solicited on Fridays compared to Mondays, reflecting subconscious associations between approaching weekends and psychological abundance mindsets. Corporate managers pitching budget proposals to executives experience 42% higher approval rates when scheduling meetings between 10:00 AM and 11:30 AM, compared to afternoon sessions—a temporal sweet spot after morning coffee has activated cognitive resources but before lunch-related glucose depletion impairs executive function. These timing effects operate without conscious recognition; executives don't think "I'm approving this because it's 10:47 AM," yet their neural state at that moment creates receptivity that the same proposal at 3:15 PM wouldn't generate.

The strategic sequencing of information and experiences creates what researchers call "unconscious priming cascades," in which early stimuli shape the interpretation of subsequent information without an explicit connection. Marketing researchers studying automobile showrooms discovered that salespeople who begin customer interactions by discussing the vehicle's most expensive optional features—premium sound systems, advanced safety packages, luxury interior upgrades—subsequently close sales on higher-tier base models compared to colleagues who present vehicles in ascending price order. The mechanism involves subconscious anchoring: exposure to twenty-thousand-dollar option packages makes a forty-five-thousand-dollar vehicle feel relatively moderate by comparison, even though that exact vehicle would feel expensive if presented first. The customer never consciously thinks "I was primed to accept higher prices," yet the priming sequence reliably influences willingness to pay. This phenomenon explains why luxury brands deliberately showcase their most extravagant products prominently—the limited-edition twelve-thousand-dollar handbag displayed in the window makes the four-hundred-dollar bags inside feel almost reasonable by comparison, even though four hundred dollars objectively represents substantial expenditure for most consumers.

Temporal spacing of repeated exposures exploits unconscious memory consolidation processes to enhance persuasive message retention without triggering conscious resistance. Neuroscientists studying memory formation identify optimal spacing intervals for information exposure: material presented three times over one week generates 47% stronger memory encoding than three exposures in a single day, because spaced repetition allows neural consolidation during intervening periods. Political campaigns exploit this research by scheduling ad exposures using algorithms that optimize spacing—not so frequent as to cause conscious annoyance, but distributed across intervals that maximize unconscious familiarity without triggering conscious recognition of manipulation. Voters who see a candidate's message three times weekly across four weeks develop stronger positive associations than those receiving twelve concentrated exposures in one week, despite identical total exposure. The distributed pattern feels less like bombardment and more like natural environmental presence, bypassing the defensive reactions that conscious recognition of persuasion attempts typically activate.

Sensory Persuasion Beyond Vision

While visual stimuli dominate discussions of persuasion, olfactory stimuli operate through neural pathways that provide uniquely direct access to emotional and memory centers, creating powerful subconscious associations that visual stimuli cannot match. The olfactory bulb connects directly to the amygdala and hippocampus—brain structures central to emotional processing and memory formation—without routing through the thalamus, as other sensory information must. This anatomical reality means scents trigger emotional responses and memories before conscious interpretation occurs. Real estate agents who bake cookies or brew coffee before open houses aren't simply creating pleasant atmospheres; they're activating unconscious associations between home comfort and the property being shown. Research measuring offer prices from prospective buyers reveals that properties scented with baking aromas receive offers that are, on average, 4% higher than identical properties without scent enhancement. Buyers don't consciously calculate "I smell cookies, therefore I'll bid more"; instead, the olfactory experience triggers unconscious warmth and comfort associations that translate into increased perceived property value.

Luxury retailers have industrialized olfactory persuasion through signature scent strategies that create unconscious brand associations. Abercrombie & Fitch's distinctive "Fierce" fragrance, Singapore Airlines' "Stefan Floridian Waters" cabin scent, and Westin Hotels' "White Tea" aroma function as olfactory logos—distinctive scent signatures that become unconsciously associated with brand identity. Neuroimaging studies tracking customers exposed to these signature scents reveal heightened activation in brain regions related to brand recognition and positive affect compared to unscented competitor environments. The mechanism operates bidirectionally: experiencing the scent in-store strengthens brand associations that later scent encounters reactivate, while remembering the brand unconsciously triggers olfactory memories even in the absence of scent. A business traveler passing Abercrombie & Fitch in an airport unconsciously experiences a brief activation of scent memories that reinforce the brand's presence, even though they never enter the store. This olfactory persuasion operates entirely outside conscious awareness; customers rarely explicitly notice or discuss brand scents, yet these aromas reliably influence purchasing behavior and brand loyalty.

Sonic persuasion through carefully designed soundscapes exploits psychoacoustic principles that influence emotion, perception, and behavior without conscious recognition.

Restaurants employ acoustic consultants who optimize ambient sound levels, music tempo, and frequency distributions to influence dining pace and revenue. Research across multiple restaurant types demonstrates that faster-tempo music increases table turnover by reducing average dining time by 17%, while slower tempos encourage lingering, increasing beverage orders by 23%. The effect operates unconsciously: diners don't think "this music is fast, I should eat quickly," yet their behavioral pace unconsciously synchronizes with musical tempo. High-end restaurants targeting maximum per-table revenue strategically employ slower classical music during peak hours, while high-volume casual dining chains optimize turnover with uptempo popular music. The sonic environment persuades by establishing unconscious behavioral rhythms that customers follow without recognizing the mechanism of influence.

The strategic use of silence represents perhaps the most counterintuitive sonic persuasion tool, exploiting psychological discomfort with auditory voids to influence behavior. Luxury retailers like Apple Store deliberately maintain minimal background sound, creating acoustic environments where product interactions and sales conversations dominate the sensory landscape. This silence serves multiple persuasive functions: it positions products as worthy of focused attention rather than background accompaniment, it creates slight psychological pressure that encourages shorter browsing periods and faster purchase decisions, and it makes the acoustic experience of using products—the click of a laptop keyboard, the swipe sound of a tablet—more perceptually prominent. Researchers measuring browsing-to-purchase conversion rates find that Apple's relatively silent stores result in purchase decisions 9% faster than those in traditional electronics retailers with constant background music. The silence persuades by creating an acoustic space that unconsciously elevates product interactions above mere shopping to something more significant.

Digital Interfaces and Unconscious Behavioral Engineering

The digital persuasion landscape has evolved sophisticated techniques for influencing behavior through interface design choices that exploit unconscious cognitive patterns and motor habits. Variable ratio reinforcement schedules—the exact mechanism that makes slot machines addictive—now power social media engagement through unpredictable notification patterns and content feeds. When users check their social media applications, they encounter uncertain rewards: sometimes new messages await, engaging content appears, and sometimes nothing noteworthy is there. This unpredictability elicits unconscious dopamine responses that are significantly more powerful than those produced by predictable rewards. Neuroscientists using PET scans to measure dopamine release during variable-reward tasks document 43% higher activation than during fixed-reward schedules, explaining why users compulsively check applications dozens of times daily, despite most checks yielding nothing valuable. Persuasion operates through neurochemical mechanisms that bypass conscious decision-making; users don't consciously decide "I want unpredictable dopamine hits," yet their behavior reliably follows patterns engineered by these reward schedules.

Interface friction—the effort required to complete actions—represents another vector for unconscious behavioral engineering that platforms manipulate to influence user behavior. Social media applications make content consumption nearly frictionless through infinite scrolling that requires minimal motor effort, while deliberately increasing friction for account deletion by requiring multiple confirmation steps, waiting periods, and maze-like navigation settings. This asymmetric friction distribution exploits unconscious effort-minimization tendencies: users unconsciously follow paths of least resistance without explicitly weighing whether they want to keep scrolling. Research tracking eye movements and interaction patterns reveals that reducing the number of action completions from 3 to 2 increases completion rates by 27%, while adding just one additional confirmation step decreases completion rates by 19%. These effects compound by making desired behaviors frictionless and undesired behaviors effortful; platforms guide user behavior through unconscious effort calculations that users never explicitly articulate to themselves.

Default settings constitute perhaps the most powerful yet ethically contentious form of digital subconscious persuasion, exploiting status quo bias—the unconscious preference for maintaining the current state over changing it. When applications default to maximum data sharing, automatic renewal subscriptions, or opt-in marketing communications, they harness unconscious inertia that keeps users in default configurations despite preferences they would express if forced to choose consciously. Behavioral economists studying default effects across multiple domains document that defaults determine outcomes in seventy to ninety-five percent of cases, depending on context, even when switching requires minimal effort. Organ donation rates illustrate this power dramatically: countries with opt-out donation defaults (where citizens must actively choose not to donate) show donation rates above 90%. In comparison, opt-in default countries rarely exceed 20% participation despite similar cultural attitudes toward donation. The default persuades by positioning one option as the path of least cognitive and motor effort, exploiting unconscious preference for avoiding decisions rather than making them.

Color Psychology and Unconscious Association Networks

Color selections in persuasive contexts activate unconscious association networks developed through evolutionary history and cultural conditioning, influencing perception and behavior through mechanisms that conscious reasoning cannot easily override. Red, across diverse human cultures, triggers unconscious arousal and urgency responses— physiological reactions including a slightly elevated heart rate, increased skin conductance, and enhanced attention. Retailers exploit these unconscious, red-triggered responses through sale signs, clearance tags, and limited-time offer promotions that leverage red's evolutionary associations with danger and urgency. A/B testing across thousands of e-commerce sites reveals that red "Buy Now" buttons generate nine to twelve percent higher click-through rates compared to other colors, not because customers consciously think "red means urgent," but because red triggers unconscious arousal that translates into action bias. The color persuades by activating physiological states conducive to the desired behavior without requiring conscious mediation.

Blue's persuasive power operates through opposite mechanisms, activating unconscious associations with trust, stability, and competence. Financial institutions and technology companies disproportionately employ blue in branding because decades of psychological research document that blue triggers unconscious trust responses more reliably than other colors. When experimental subjects evaluate identical product descriptions accompanied by different-colored logos, blue-branded products receive 15%

higher trust ratings, despite color being logically irrelevant to product quality. The mechanism reflects both evolutionary heritage—blue's association with clear skies and clean water signalled safety in ancestral environments—and modern cultural conditioning, where authority institutions — from police uniforms to national flags to corporate logos — consistently employ blue. These layered associations create unconscious trust responses that conscious reasoning struggles to override, even when explicitly told color shouldn't influence judgment. The persuasion operates in the gap between what people know rationally and what they feel automatically.

Cultural variations in color associations complicate the universal deployment of color-based persuasion, requiring a sophisticated understanding of context-dependent unconscious responses. While white triggers unconscious purity and cleanliness associations in Western contexts, many East Asian cultures associate white with mourning and death, creating opposite unconscious emotional responses. A Western healthcare brand employing white packaging to signal hygiene might trigger unconscious discomfort in Asian markets where these associations differ. Similarly, red's positive associations with prosperity and celebration in Chinese culture contrast with Western contexts, where red sometimes signals danger or financial losses. Effective persuaders recognize that color-triggered unconscious responses aren't hardwired universally but rather reflect culturally learned patterns that vary systematically across populations. Global brands increasingly employ color consultants who map these cultural variation patterns to optimize unconscious color responses for specific market contexts.

The strategic combination of colors generates emergent unconscious effects beyond what individual colors produce.

Fast food chains overwhelmingly employ red-and-yellow color schemes because research in appetite psychology reveals this combination unconsciously stimulates hunger responses while accelerating perceived time passage. The red component triggers arousal and urgency, the yellow enhances these effects while adding cheerfulness associations, and their combination creates unconscious restlessness that encourages faster eating and quicker departure—ideal for high-turnover business models. Neuroimaging research tracking brain responses to color combinations reveals that specific pairings activate reward-processing regions more intensely than either color alone, suggesting non-additive interaction effects in which combinations elicit unique unconscious reactions. McDonald's, KFC, Burger King, In-N-Out, and dozens of other fast food brands converge on similar red-yellow color palettes not by coincidence but through systematic testing that reveals these combinations' unconscious influence on eating behavior and turnover rates.

Priming Effects and Behavioral Contagion

Unconscious priming—where exposure to stimuli influences subsequent behavior without awareness of the connection—represents one of social psychology's most robust findings and most powerful persuasion mechanisms. Classic research by psychologist John Bargh demonstrated that experimental subjects exposed to words associated with elderly stereotypes (retirement, Florida, wrinkles, bingo) subsequently walked more slowly down hallways than control subjects, despite no conscious awareness of the prime or of the connection between word exposure and walking speed. This finding launched thousands of priming studies revealing that unconscious exposure to concepts, images, or environmental cues reliably influences subsequent behavior across domains from consumer choices to moral judgments to academic performance. When students complete math tests in rooms decorated with images of Albert Einstein and other intellectual icons, their scores average 8% higher than identical tests in neutral rooms—an effect researchers term "genius priming," in which unconscious activation of intelligence-related concepts enhances actual cognitive performance.

Commercial persuaders have industrialized priming through strategic environmental and communicative elements designed to activate desired unconscious associations. Luxury brands prime affluence and exclusivity through velvet ropes, security guards, and deliberately intimidating retail environments that unconsciously activate wealth-related concepts. Research tracking purchasing behavior reveals that these environmental primes influence not just whether customers buy but what they purchase: exposure to luxury primes increases selection of higher-priced options within product lines by seventeen to twenty-four percent. The mechanism operates through temporary accessibility effects—luxury environmental cues make wealth-related concepts more cognitively accessible, creating unconscious frameworks through which subsequent decisions are filtered. Customers don't think, "I was primed for luxury, therefore I'll buy the expensive version"; instead, the expensive option feels more appropriate, in a way they cannot articulate, because the prime-behavior connection operates outside conscious awareness.

Behavioral contagion is a related phenomenon in which observing others' behavior unconsciously influences one's own actions through automatic mimicry and social coordination mechanisms. When hotel guests find cards in their rooms stating "the majority of guests in this room reuse towels," towel reuse rates increase by thirty-three percent compared to generic environmental appeals—a striking example of how behavioral observation (even reported rather than directly witnessed) unconsciously influences action. The mechanism reflects deeply embedded social coordination instincts, in which automatic behavioral matching facilitated group cohesion in ancestral environments. Modern persuaders exploit these instincts by strategically displaying desired behaviors: restaurants seed tip jars with bills rather than coins to prime larger denominations, streaming services display "trending now" designations to trigger bandwagon effects, and retailers position products with "bestseller" badges to activate social proof mechanisms that operate unconsciously.

The power of behavioral contagion extends to emotional states through unconscious mimicry of facial expressions and body language. When service workers display genuine smiles characterized by orbicularis oculi muscle activation around the eyes—so-called "Duchenne smiles" that distinguish authentic from posed expressions—customers unconsciously mirror these expressions through automatic facial mimicry, triggering corresponding emotional states through proprioceptive feedback. This emotional contagion occurs within milliseconds—faster than conscious emotion recognition—and reliably influences customer satisfaction ratings and tipping behavior. Research using high-speed video analysis reveals that authentic smiles from servers increase tips by an average of eighteen percent compared to posed smiles or neutral expressions, demonstrating how unconscious emotional synchronization creates measurable behavioral outcomes. The persuasion happens not through conscious thought—"this person is smiling, therefore I should tip more"—but through automatic emotional contagion that operates beneath awareness.

The recognition that most persuasion operates through subconscious mechanisms rather than conscious argumentation transforms how ethically responsible influence agents approach their work. Rather than viewing persuasion exclusively as rational discourse where superior arguments prevail, sophisticated persuaders recognize they're designing comprehensive experiences that shape behavior through environmental architecture, sensory stimuli, temporal sequencing, and unconscious priming. This expanded view demands heightened ethical attention because subconscious influence bypasses the conscious deliberation that provides traditional protection against manipulation. When persuasion operated primarily through explicit claims that audiences could consciously evaluate, ethical guidelines focused on truthfulness, logical validity, and transparent intentions. When persuasion increasingly operates through mechanisms audiences cannot consciously detect or resist, ethical frameworks must expand to address this asymmetric awareness—persuaders who understand the influence mechanisms they're employing while audiences remain unaware these mechanisms are at work. The most principled persuaders recognize this asymmetry and impose self-restraint proportional to their influence sophistication, ensuring that subconscious persuasion serves authentic value creation rather than exploitative manipulation.

Chapter 8: The Ethics of Persuasion: Balancing Influence and Integrity

When Cambridge Analytica harvested the personal data of eighty-seven million Facebook users without consent to construct psychographic profiles for political advertising during the 2016 election cycle, they deployed persuasion techniques of unprecedented sophistication—and created an ethical catastrophe that would ultimately destroy the company. Their algorithms could identify which voters experienced high neuroticism, low openness to experience, or specific anxiety triggers, then serve customized messages exploiting these psychological vulnerabilities. A single parent struggling financially might receive targeted advertisements emphasizing threats to economic security, while a voter concerned about social order encountered messages amplifying fear of cultural change. The technical achievement was remarkable; each message reached precisely the audience most psychologically susceptible to its particular emotional appeal. Yet this precision targeting raised fundamental questions that extend far beyond one scandal: When does persuasion cross from legitimate influence into manipulation? What responsibilities do persuaders bear toward those they seek to influence? How should we distinguish between ethical persuasion that respects human autonomy and coercive techniques that exploit psychological vulnerabilities? These questions have become urgent as advancing technology enables influence strategies that previous generations could never have imagined, creating ethical challenges that existing moral frameworks struggle to address.

The ethical dimensions of persuasion have always existed, but they've grown exponentially more complex as our understanding of human psychology deepens and our technological capabilities expand. Ancient rhetoricians debated whether sophistic techniques constituted legitimate argumentation or dangerous trickery; today, we confront persuasion environments where artificial intelligence can generate thousands of personalized messages simultaneously, each calibrated to exploit specific cognitive biases in target audiences. Neuroimaging reveals which message framings activate reward centers most intensely, eye-tracking identifies which visual elements capture attention most effectively, and behavioral economics provides detailed maps of decision-making vulnerabilities waiting to be exploited. This knowledge empowers persuaders with influence capabilities that approach the sophistication of mental manipulation. The fundamental ethical question is no longer whether we possess tools capable of overwhelming rational judgment—we clearly do— but rather how persuaders should exercise the considerable power these tools provide. Creating ethical frameworks for modern persuasion requires grappling with the uncomfortable reality that effectiveness and ethics don't naturally align; the most powerful persuasion techniques often raise the most serious ethical concerns.

The Autonomy Principle: Respecting Human Agency

At the foundation of ethical persuasion lies respect for human autonomy—the recognition that people possess fundamental rights to make decisions based on their own values, interests, and reasoning without being manipulated through deception or psychological coercion. Philosopher Immanuel Kant articulated this principle through his categorical imperative, arguing that treating people as mere means to our ends rather than as ends in themselves violates their fundamental dignity as rational agents. Applied to persuasion, this framework suggests that ethical influence must preserve the target's capacity for genuine choice. When a persuader uses transparent argumentation that allows audiences to evaluate claims on their merits, they respect autonomy by enabling informed decision-making. When they deploy techniques designed to bypass rational evaluation—exploiting fears they know to be exaggerated, triggering emotional responses disconnected from legitimate concerns, or withholding information necessary for sound judgment—they treat audiences as objects to be manipulated rather than persons to be respected.

The autonomy principle generates concrete guidelines that distinguish ethical from problematic persuasion. First, ethical persuaders maintain truthfulness not merely in the narrow technical sense of avoiding explicit falsehoods, but in the broader sense of providing information that accurately represents reality without strategic omissions designed to mislead. A pharmaceutical company promoting a medication might technically avoid lying by listing side effects in dense, technical language buried in fine print. Yet, this practice violates the spirit of truth-telling by deliberately obscuring risks that should inform patient decisions. Second, ethical persuasion respects audience capacity for rational evaluation by presenting arguments that engage conscious reasoning rather than exclusively targeting subconscious processes that bypass deliberative thought. Indeed, all persuasion involves emotional and non-rational elements—humans aren't pure logic machines—but ethical approaches balance emotional appeals with substantive argumentation that gives audiences genuine opportunities to assess claims critically. Third, ethical persuaders avoid exploiting known cognitive vulnerabilities in ways that predictably produce decisions contrary to the audience's authentic interests and values. Everyone experiences cognitive biases, but deliberately weaponizing these against people's well-being crosses from influence into manipulation.

The transparency test provides a practical method for evaluating whether persuasion techniques respect autonomy: would the techniques remain effective if thoroughly explained to the audience beforehand? If a salesperson told prospects, "I'm going to create artificial scarcity by claiming limited availability to trigger your fear of missing out, even though abundant inventory exists," the technique would lose effectiveness immediately. This failure under transparency signals that the approach relies on deception or exploitation rather than legitimate influence. Contrast this with a nonprofit fundraiser who explains, "I'll share stories of individuals helped by our programs because research shows that concrete narratives generate a stronger emotional connection than abstract statistics, and we want you to understand the human impact of donations." This transparency doesn't undermine the storytelling's effectiveness because the technique doesn't depend on audiences remaining ignorant of its operation. Ethical persuaders should be able to defend their methods publicly without requiring audiences to remain unaware of the strategies they employ. This standard doesn't mean persuaders must constantly explain their techniques—that would be tedious and impractical—but rather that their approaches should withstand scrutiny rather than dissolving when exposed to light.

The Vulnerability Gradient: Differential Ethical Obligations

Ethical responsibilities intensify dramatically when persuasion targets populations experiencing heightened vulnerability due to age, cognitive capacity, emotional state, or power differentials. Children represent the most transparent case: their developing prefrontal cortexes, limited life experience, and incomplete understanding of persuasive intent create cognitive vulnerabilities that ethical persuaders must acknowledge through enhanced protections. This recognition underlies regulations restricting advertising to children, prohibiting practices like embedding product placements in educational content or using cartoon characters to promote unhealthy foods. The ethical logic extends beyond legal compliance to a broader principle: when audiences lack fully developed capacities for evaluating persuasive appeals, persuaders bear heightened responsibility to avoid exploitation. Research on adolescent brain development reveals that regions governing impulse control and long-term consequence evaluation don't fully mature until the mid-twenties, suggesting ethical obligations extend beyond childhood into young adulthood for persuasion involving significant commitments or risks.

Emotional vulnerability creates another category that demands heightened ethical care. People experiencing grief, trauma, fear, or other intensely destabilizing emotions show measurably impaired decision-making capacity. Neuroscientific studies using fMRI during emotional distress demonstrate reduced activity in prefrontal regions associated with rational evaluation alongside heightened activity in amygdala regions linked to threat response and impulsive action. Someone who just lost a spouse to cancer shows dramatically different susceptibility to persuasive appeals about experimental treatments, alternative medicines, or financial decisions compared to their baseline cognitive state. Ethical persuaders in such contexts face a choice: they can exploit emotional vulnerability to maximize immediate influence, or they can exercise restraint, recognizing that decisions made during acute emotional distress frequently contradict people's settled values and long-term interests.

Financial advisors who aggressively market investment products to recent widows, funeral homes that upsell expensive casket options to grieving families, or disaster-area contractors who pressure traumatized homeowners into immediate renovation contracts all demonstrate the ethical abandonment that occurs when persuaders prioritize their interests over vulnerable audiences' genuine welfare.

Power asymmetries compound vulnerability through information advantages, resource disparities, and unequal consequences for decision errors. When pharmaceutical companies market directly to physicians, the relationship involves professionals with relatively balanced expertise and institutional protections. When those same companies market to patients lacking medical knowledge, facing serious illness, and experiencing legitimate desperation, the power dynamics shift profoundly. Patients cannot independently evaluate complex pharmacological claims, face potentially catastrophic consequences from poor treatment choices, and often experience emotional states that impair judgment. Ethical pharmaceutical marketing to patients, therefore, requires substantially more restraint than marketing to medical professionals—more conservative claims, more transparent risk communication, stronger encouragement to consult physicians, and scrupulous avoidance of exploiting fear or desperation. Similar principles apply across domains: employers hold power advantages over job applicants, professors over students, police over suspects, landlords over housing applicants, and creditors over borrowers. These asymmetries create the potential for coercion, where what appears to be persuasion actually reflects pressure that audiences cannot realistically resist. Ethical influence in such contexts requires persuaders to acknowledge power differentials and to compensate by enhancing transparency, reducing pressure tactics, and genuinely respecting audience decisions, including refusal.

The vulnerability gradient generates what ethicists call "special obligations"—responsibilities that intensify based on target audience characteristics rather than remaining constant across contexts. A retailer marketing luxury goods to affluent consumers operates under different ethical constraints than a payday lender targeting economically desperate borrowers, not because the persuasion techniques differ but because the vulnerability and consequences differ dramatically. The luxury retailer persuading someone to purchase an expensive watch causes minimal harm, even if the buyer later regrets the expenditure; the payday lender persuading someone into a loan with a 400% annual interest rate can trigger a debt spiral with devastating consequences. Ethical persuasion, therefore, requires contextual analysis that considers audience vulnerability, decision stakes, power dynamics, and potential harms rather than applying uniform standards regardless of circumstances. This variability creates complexity—there's no simple checklist that determines ethical appropriateness across all situations—but that complexity reflects genuine moral reality rather than fuzzy thinking.

The Consent Paradox: Voluntary Exposure to Influence

Modern persuasion increasingly operates through platforms and environments that audiences voluntarily enter, creating complex questions about consent and responsibility. When someone downloads a free social media application, visits a retail website, or subscribes to an email newsletter, they knowingly expose themselves to persuasive messaging. Service providers argue that this voluntary participation constitutes implicit consent to persuasion attempts. Users clicked "agree" to the terms of service (however lengthy and legalistic), chose to visit platforms funded by advertising, and could exit at any time. From this perspective, ethical obligations diminish because audiences actively opt into persuasion environments rather than having influence imposed involuntarily. This consent argument appears particularly strong for sophisticated audiences—adults with education, internet experience, and awareness that free services involve data collection and targeted advertising. Nobody forces them to use Facebook, Instagram, or TikTok; they make autonomous choices weighing platform benefits against privacy and persuasion costs.

However, this consent framework faces serious challenges that complicate its moral clarity. First, meaningful consent requires adequate information about what one is consenting to, yet persuasion platforms deliberately obscure the sophistication and extent of their influence techniques. Terms of service mention data collection without explaining that behavioral tracking enables psychological profiling more detailed than what clinical psychologists produce through extensive patient interviews. Users might understand intellectually that platforms use "personalization." Still, they cannot grasp that algorithms track thousands of behavioral signals to model their specific susceptibilities, then exploit these models through influence techniques calibrated to individual psychology. Without understanding what they're actually consenting to, users cannot provide truly informed consent. Second, voluntary participation becomes questionable when platforms achieve such market dominance that opting out imposes significant social and professional costs. If job networking requires LinkedIn participation, professional visibility demands Twitter engagement, and social connection necessitates Facebook membership, describing these as "voluntary choices" mischaracterizes the realistic alternatives. Theoretically, people can refuse; practically, they face substantial disadvantages that make refusal so costly that it calls into question whether participation truly reflects free choice.

Third, the consent argument treats initial platform adoption as the relevant decision point while ignoring that persuasion sophistication escalates continuously after users join. Someone who agreed to Facebook's terms in 2007 consented to a platform with primitive targeting compared to contemporary capabilities involving artificial intelligence, predictive modeling, and real-time behavioral optimization. The persuasion environment they actually experience bears little resemblance to the one that existed when they initially consented. Yet, platforms operate under legal frameworks that treat initial consent as perpetually valid regardless of how radically the bargain changes. This creates what legal scholars term "rolling contracts," where the actual terms of exchange evolve continually without opportunities for meaningful renegotiation. Users can theoretically leave, but doing so requires abandoning accumulated social connections, content libraries, and network effects that represent substantial investments. The switching costs mean that staying doesn't necessarily signal ongoing consent to new persuasion practices; rather, it reflects the prohibitive expense of exit.

These consent complications generate profound ethical implications for persuaders operating through platforms where participation appears voluntary but actually involves constrained choice, inadequate information, and evolving terms. Ethical platforms would provide genuinely transparent information about persuasion techniques in language accessible to typical users rather than legalistic obscurity. They would enable meaningful control, including options to turn off behavioral tracking, algorithmic personalization, and psychological targeting, rather than offering only an all-or-nothing choice between complete exposure and complete platform abandonment. They would recognize that even when users technically consent to data collection, ethical obligations persist regarding how that data gets used. The fact that someone shared information doesn't automatically justify every conceivable application; implied consent has limits that ethical persuaders should respect, even when legal frameworks don't mandate such restraint. Most fundamentally, ethical platforms would acknowledge that power asymmetries between sophisticated technology companies and individual users create special obligations regardless of consent, because meaningful consent requires more balanced information and power than currently exists.

Professional Codes and Industry Self-Regulation

Many persuasion-intensive professions have developed ethical codes attempting to establish standards distinguishing legitimate practice from manipulation or exploitation. The American Marketing Association's code of ethics prohibits deliberately misleading advertising, requires clear disclosure of paid endorsements, and mandates respect for consumer privacy preferences. The Public Relations Society of America commits its members to honest communication, the protection of confidential information, and the avoidance of conflicts of interest that would compromise independent judgment. Medical professional associations restrict pharmaceutical marketing to physicians through guidelines that limit gift values, require scientific accuracy in promotional claims, and prohibit inducements that would distort prescribing decisions. These codes reflect professional recognition that unconstrained persuasion — pursuing maximum effectiveness regardless of consequences — ultimately damages both public welfare and professional legitimacy. By establishing ethical boundaries, professions attempt to maintain social license while preserving self-governance rather than inviting external regulation.

However, professional self-regulation faces inherent limitations that question its adequacy for ensuring ethical persuasion. First, codes typically establish minimum standards rather than aspirational ideals, defining unacceptable practices while leaving substantial latitude for ethically questionable approaches that don't technically violate explicit prohibitions. A code might forbid outright deception while remaining silent about sophisticated framing techniques that mislead through implication and omission rather than explicit falsehood. Second, enforcement mechanisms often prove weak because professional associations lack subpoena power, regulatory authority, and resources for systematic compliance monitoring. Violations might trigger membership revocation, but this sanction matters only if professional association membership significantly affects career prospects—a condition that holds for physicians and lawyers but not for marketers or public relations practitioners who can practice without association affiliation. Third, competitive pressures create a prisoner's dilemma in which individual practitioners who restrain themselves lose business to less scrupulous competitors, gradually eroding ethical standards as a survival strategy. If aggressive persuaders who exploit vulnerabilities and test ethical boundaries gain market share. At the same time, cautious practitioners who exercise restraint lose clients, and the profession collectively drifts toward more problematic practices regardless of stated ethical commitments.

Industry self-regulation faces additional challenges from financial incentives that reward ethical violations when gains exceed expected sanction costs. Pharmaceutical companies that illegally market drugs for unapproved uses, social media platforms that exploit user data beyond consent boundaries, or financial institutions that deploy predatory lending practices can calculate whether the profits from violations exceed anticipated fines, reputational damage, and legal expenses. When violations generate billions in revenue while penalties amount to millions, the incentive structure encourages ethical breaches as calculated business risks rather than deterring them as unacceptable transgressions. This cost-benefit calculation explains patterns where companies systematically violate ethical standards, absorb penalties as business costs, and continue problematic practices because fundamental incentives remain unchanged. Effective ethical governance requires either sanctions severe enough that the expected costs exceed the benefits of the violation, or structural reforms that align financial incentives with ethical behavior rather than creating tensions between profitability and integrity.

The limitations of professional self-regulation suggest that external accountability mechanisms—including regulatory oversight, legal liability, and public transparency—provide necessary complements to voluntary ethical codes. Regulations such as the Federal Trade Commission's truth-in-advertising requirements, the Food and Drug Administration's pharmaceutical marketing restrictions, and the European Union's General Data Protection Regulation set legal boundaries that professions must respect, regardless of voluntary commitments. Legal liability for harms caused by deceptive or manipulative persuasion establishes financial consequences that influence cost-benefit calculations more effectively than purely ethical considerations. Public transparency through investigative journalism, academic research, and advocacy organizations exposes problematic practices that might otherwise remain hidden, creating reputation costs and public pressure that supplement professional discipline. These external mechanisms don't replace professional ethics but rather establish baseline standards and accountability systems that support ethical practice by reducing the competitive advantage of unscrupulous actors.

Developing Personal Ethical Frameworks for Persuasive Practice

Individual persuaders must ultimately develop personal ethical frameworks to guide their professional conduct, because institutional codes, regulations, and industry standards cannot address every situation or resolve every moral dilemma. These frameworks should begin with honest reflection about underlying values and commitments. What principles matter enough that violating them would feel intolerable regardless of professional consequences? What obligations do persuaders owe audiences beyond avoiding legal violations? How should persuaders balance their legitimate interests in career success and financial security against responsibilities toward those they influence? These foundational questions don't admit universal answers applicable across all persons and contexts, but grappling with them forces explicit articulation of moral commitments rather than drifting through ethical decisions based on convenience or rationalization. Research on moral development reveals that people rarely engage in conscious ethical deliberation before acting; instead, they make rapid, intuitive judgments and then construct post hoc justifications. Creating explicit ethical frameworks before confronting challenging situations enables more considered moral judgment by establishing principles that can guide decisions in moments when intuitive responses might serve self-interest rather than genuine ethics.

Practical ethical frameworks should include decision procedures for situations that present moral uncertainty rather than clear right-or-wrong answers. The publicity test asks whether persuaders would feel comfortable having their techniques and reasoning publicly disclosed and evaluated by people they respect. If a persuasion strategy requires secrecy to remain effective or would generate shame if exposed, that signals ethical problems warranting reconsideration. The reversibility test asks whether persuaders would consider their approach acceptable if they were the target rather than the source. When financial advisors recommend investment products, would they want similar recommendations for their own parents, based on the same reasoning? If not, the discrepancy suggests their judgments prioritize their commissions over client interests. The stakeholder test systematically considers the impacts on everyone affected by persuasive outcomes—not just the immediate target and persuader, but also indirect parties who experience consequences. A pharmaceutical company marketing an expensive medication should consider not only prescribing physicians and shareholders, but also patients bearing costs, insurers funding treatments, and healthcare systems experiencing resource constraints.

Ethical frameworks should also specify personal boundaries— practices that persuaders categorically refuse regardless of legality or industry norms. These boundaries might include prohibitions on targeting children irrespective of product type, absolute honesty requirements even when omission would be legally permissible, or refusal to employ techniques that deliberately trigger addictive behaviors. Such bright lines simplify decisions by eliminating specific options from consideration rather than weighing them against competing factors. They also foster personal integrity, protecting against gradual ethical erosion through repeated small compromises that cumulatively drift toward practices the persuader would initially have considered unacceptable. Research on moral slippery slopes demonstrates that people who make minor ethical concessions progressively rationalize larger transgressions, each justified as only slightly beyond the previous boundary. Establishing categorical prohibitions interrupts this drift by defining specific actions as absolutely unacceptable rather than leaving them to situational judgment.

Finally, robust ethical frameworks embrace ongoing learning and reflection rather than treating moral development as complete. Persuasion techniques, technologies, and contexts evolve continuously, generating novel ethical challenges that existing frameworks may not adequately address. The emergence of deepfake videos that depict people saying things they never said, artificial intelligence that can generate personalized messages at scale, and neurotechnology that could enable direct brain stimulation for persuasive purposes raises ethical questions that previous generations never confronted. Ethical persuaders should actively engage with scholarship examining these developments, participate in professional discussions about appropriate boundaries, and regularly reassess their practices in light of new understanding. They should seek feedback from trusted colleagues on the ethical dimensions of their work, particularly from those outside their immediate professional context who might spot problems that insiders overlook. Most importantly, they should approach ethical reflection with genuine openness rather than defensiveness, recognizing that moral wisdom develops through confronting uncomfortable questions rather than avoiding them.

The path toward ethical persuasion requires continuous effort and honest self-examination rather than following simple rules or avoiding apparent violations. It demands balancing effectiveness and integrity when these values conflict, accepting professional costs when ethical boundaries preclude the use of maximally powerful techniques, and recognizing that persuasion always involves exercising power over others—a responsibility that should inspire humility rather than entitlement. The most sophisticated technical knowledge about influence strategies ultimately means little if persuaders lack moral wisdom to deploy these capabilities responsibly. Conversely, strong ethical intentions accomplish limited good without understanding how persuasion actually operates and what techniques raise genuine concerns. Mastery requires integrating moral philosophy with psychological understanding, recognizing that ethics and effectiveness represent complementary rather than competing dimensions of persuasive excellence. Those who achieve this integration don't merely influence people successfully; they affect them in ways that respect human dignity, preserve autonomy, and contribute to rather than corrupt human flourishing. That standard elevates persuasion from a merely technical skill into a genuine profession deserving of both power and trust.

Chapter 9: Digital Persuasion: Navigating the Online World

When TikTok's algorithm recommended a video about intermittent fasting to Marcus, a forty-two-year-old accountant who had never searched for diet content, he watched thirty seconds before scrolling past. The next day, another fasting video appeared. Then another. Within two weeks, Marcus had watched 47 videos on the topic, downloaded a fasting app, purchased supplements from an Instagram ad, and joined an online community where strangers praised his "transformation" despite having changed nothing yet. He never consciously decided to adopt this lifestyle change. The decision emerged gradually through an accumulation of micro-exposures, each too brief to trigger critical evaluation, collectively overwhelming his initial disinterest through persistent repetition that felt serendipitous rather than systematic. This phenomenon—algorithmic persuasion architecture—represents perhaps the most significant evolution in influence dynamics since the invention of mass media, fundamentally restructuring how messages reach audiences, how attention distributes across competing stimuli, and how individuals construct their understanding of social reality itself.

Digital persuasion operates through mechanisms qualitatively distinct from traditional influence contexts because the medium itself actively participates in the persuasive process rather than serving as a neutral channel for human-generated messages. When a television advertisement airs, the network broadcasts it to all viewers simultaneously; persuasion succeeds or fails based on message content, creative execution, and audience receptivity. Digital platforms, by contrast, function as active intermediaries that continuously optimize which messages each individual sees, when they encounter them, and in what sequence—all calibrated by machine learning systems processing billions of behavioral data points to maximize engagement metrics. Facebook's News Feed algorithm considers approximately 100,000 factors when determining which posts appear to each user, including not just explicit preferences but also micro-behaviors like hover duration over images, scrolling velocity through different content types, and facial expressions captured by device cameras when users enable that functionality. These systems predict with eerie accuracy which content will generate clicks, shares, comments, and extended viewing time, then systematically expose users to that predicted high-engagement content while suppressing material the algorithm anticipates will generate quick scrolling or app closure.

This algorithmic curation creates persuasion environments fundamentally different from any humans evolved to navigate. Throughout human history, until approximately fifteen years ago, individuals encountered information through mechanisms that involved substantial human agency: they chose which newspapers to read, which television channels to watch, which friends to listen to, and which experts to consult. Digital platforms collapse this agency by outsourcing information discovery to algorithms whose selection criteria remain opaque and whose "choices" serve platform business models rather than user interests. Research conducted by Guillaume Chaslot, a former YouTube recommendation engineer, analyzing the platform's algorithm, found that the system systematically amplified content that maximized watch time, regardless of accuracy, quality, or social value. Videos presenting conspiracy theories, extreme political positions, or sensationalized health claims received algorithmic promotion because they generated longer viewing sessions and higher session-to-session return rates compared to factually accurate but less emotionally provocative alternatives. The algorithm wasn't programmed to prefer misinformation—it was programmed to maximize engagement, and misinformation happened to excel at generating the behavioral signals the system rewarded. Users scrolling through their feeds experienced not a representative sample of available information but rather a carefully curated collection optimized for addictiveness, creating information ecosystems where truth value became subordinate to engagement potential.

The persuasive impact of this algorithmic architecture manifests as "filter bubble radicalization"—the process by which recommendation systems gradually shift user exposure toward increasingly extreme versions of their existing preferences. Someone who watches one video questioning vaccine safety gets recommended slightly more skeptical content. Engaging with that generates recommendations for overtly anti-vaccine material. Continued interaction surfaces increasingly extreme conspiracy content, each step feeling like organic discovery rather than systematic funneling. Zeynep Tufekci's research at the University of North Carolina documenting this phenomenon found that YouTube's algorithm reliably escalated users from mainstream political content toward extreme partisan material, from jogging videos to ultra-marathon content, and from vegetarian recipes to raw vegan advocacy. The pattern was consistent: the algorithm interpreted any engagement as a signal to provide more extreme variations on the theme, creating radicalization pipelines that operated through thousands of micro-recommendations rather than single persuasive encounters. Users emerged from these algorithmic rabbit holes genuinely believing they had independently researched topics and reached conclusions through personal investigation, unaware that their information journey had been systematically curated to maximize platform engagement metrics rather than support informed understanding.

The Persuasion Asymmetry: Individual Agency Versus Computational Scale

Digital persuasion environments create unprecedented power asymmetries between persuaders and audiences because machine learning systems can simultaneously target millions of individuals with personalized messaging. At the same time, human cognitive architecture remains unchanged from pre-digital eras. When a traditional advertiser created a campaign, they developed perhaps three to five variations targeting broad demographic segments—one version for young urban professionals, another for suburban families, a third for retirees. These segments contained millions of people receiving identical messages, creating shared persuasive experiences that audiences could discuss, compare, and collectively evaluate. Digital targeting shatters this commonality. Facebook's advertising platform enables what the company calls "hyper-personalization"—the ability to target segments as narrow as one hundred people based on combinations of hundreds of variables, including location, age, interests, relationship status, education, employer, recent purchases, websites visited, apps installed, political engagement, and behavioral patterns. More importantly, advertisers can rapidly test thousands of message variations simultaneously through automated A/B testing, with algorithms identifying which specific headlines, images, emotional appeals, and calls to action generate the highest conversion rates for each microsegment, then automatically allocating advertising spend to top performers.

This computational approach to persuasion optimization generates influence dynamics that human cognition struggles to resist. Consider political advertising: a campaign using traditional media might test five different television advertisements by running them in other markets and measuring polling shifts. Digital campaigns can test 5,000 ad variations, each targeting audiences as specific as "college-educated women aged 25-34 in Wisconsin who previously expressed interest in environmental issues but haven't voted in the last two elections and recently searched for information about student loan refinancing." The system identifies that this specific audience responds most strongly to messages that frame the candidate's education policy as debt relief rather than investment in the future, feature imagery of families rather than graduates, and use a testimonial format rather than direct address. No human could consciously design such precise targeting; the optimization emerges from algorithmic processing of patterns invisible to human analysts. The persuasive advantage this creates proves nearly insurmountable for audiences, because the messages they encounter have been refined through exposure to hundreds of thousands of previous viewers, leaving only the most effective variants.

The asymmetry intensifies because digital persuasion operates continuously rather than episodically. Traditional advertising campaigns had discrete boundaries—advertisements aired during specific programs, appeared in particular publications, and occupied defined billboard spaces. Individuals could create temporal distance from persuasive messages by turning off televisions, closing magazines, or choosing routes that avoid heavy advertising. Digital persuasion colonizes all available attention through platforms designed for continuous engagement. Smartphone users check their devices an average of ninety-six times daily, according to research by screen time analytics firm RescueTime, each check exposing them to algorithmically selected content calibrated for persuasive impact. The notifications engineered to trigger these checks—Instagram likes, Facebook comments, Twitter mentions, LinkedIn connection requests—function as persuasion delivery mechanisms disguised as social interaction. Users feel they're checking messages from friends or professional contacts; actually, they're entering persuasion environments where human communications appear intermixed with promoted content, algorithmically boosted posts from brands, and sponsored messages formatted to resemble organic social interactions. The inability to create boundaries around exposure to digital persuasion creates cognitive vulnerability absent in previous media environments.

Sophisticated digital persuaders now employ what marketing technologists call "omnichannel orchestration"—coordinated messaging across multiple platforms timed to exploit specific psychological states and life circumstances. Someone searching Google for "best budget smartphones" triggers a cascade of coordinated persuasion: sponsored search results from phone manufacturers, retargeted display advertisements on news websites visited afterward, social media advertisements featuring the exact phone models searched, YouTube video suggestions reviewing those models, and email marketing if the person previously provided contact information to any related company. Each touchpoint appears independent; collectively, they create persuasive pressure through repetition across contexts that feels like social consensus rather than coordinated marketing. The phenomenon that psychologists studying online persuasion term "manufactured serendipity"—algorithmic systems that create the experience of repeatedly encountering the same brand or message through seemingly coincidental channels, generating familiarity and implicit social proof without audiences recognizing the systematic orchestration underlying these "chance" encounters.

Identity Construction and Social Performance in Digital Spaces

Digital platforms restructure persuasion by transforming private interaction into a persistent, public performance visible to extended networks. When someone posts on Facebook, writes a product review on Amazon, or comments on LinkedIn, they're not merely expressing opinions—they're constructing identity performances for audience consumption that subsequently constrain their future positions through psychological consistency pressures. This performative dimension creates novel persuasion vulnerabilities because digital communication leaves permanent records that individuals become invested in defending. Social psychologists studying online identity construction identify what they term the "documented self" phenomenon: digital platforms create externalized records of our expressed preferences, stated values, and public commitments that solidify positions initially held tentatively. Someone who publicly posts support for a particular political candidate experiences substantially stronger resistance to subsequently changing positions than someone who maintains equivalent private views without public declaration, because position reversal threatens the documented identity they've constructed through accumulated digital utterances.

Persuaders exploit this dynamic through techniques encouraging public commitment to desired positions, knowing that psychological consistency mechanisms will subsequently resist counter-persuasion. Environmental organizations ask people to post photos of themselves engaging in sustainable behaviors—using reusable bags, biking instead of driving, choosing plant-based meals— transforming private actions into public identity statements.

Once someone's social network observes them performing environmental identity, continuing that behavior pattern maintains consistency between the documented self and actual conduct. The persuasive intervention targets not just immediate behavior change but rather the construction of public identity that becomes self-reinforcing through social visibility. Marketing researchers studying this phenomenon find that consumers who publicly share brand preferences on social media exhibit 37% higher brand loyalty and 42% greater resistance to competitive advertising than consumers with equivalent private preferences but no public documentation. The mechanism operates through self-perception: we observe our public statements and infer corresponding attitudes, then experience those inferred attitudes as authentic preferences rather than recognizing their origin in performative behavior.

Digital platforms amplify identity-based persuasion through features enabling quantified social validation. The architecture of likes, shares, retweets, and upvotes transforms subjective agreement into numerical metrics that provide immediate feedback on which identity performances generate social approval. Someone posting political opinions monitors engagement metrics to assess which framings resonate with their network, unconsciously calibrating future expressions toward high-engagement positions regardless of whether those positions reflect carefully considered beliefs. Research by communication scholar Jenny Davis examining Twitter discourse found that users shifted their expressed political positions toward more extreme variants over time, with the magnitude of shift correlating with engagement metrics on previous posts. High-engagement posts—those generating substantial likes and retweets—pulled subsequent expressions in the same ideological direction because the quantified validation reinforced those positions. Low-engagement posts prompted users to adopt different framings that might elicit stronger responses. This dynamic creates algorithmic pressure toward performative extremism: moderate positions generate limited engagement, while provocative statements attract attention, with engagement metrics functioning as persuasion feedback loops that reward positions optimized for virality rather than accuracy or nuance.

The collapsed context of digital communication—where professional contacts, family members, old classmates, and casual acquaintances all share the same audience—creates additional persuasion vulnerabilities through challenges in audience management. Traditional persuasion occurred in defined contexts with distinct audiences: we presented different aspects of identity to colleagues, friends, and family, tailoring messages to each audience's expectations and values. Social media platforms collapse these contexts, forcing users to perform a unified identity across disparate audiences simultaneously. This collapse creates vulnerability because persuaders can exploit cross-context inconsistencies. Political campaigns mining social media history identify past statements that contradict current positions, using discovered inconsistencies to undermine credibility. Employers reviewing applicants' social media profiles reject candidates whose online identities suggest they are incompatible with the corporate culture. The persistent visibility of digital identity performances means that persuasive messages crafted for one audience remain permanently available for other audiences to evaluate, creating authenticity pressures that constrain future resistance to persuasion.

The Misinformation Ecosystem: Virality Mechanics and Epistemic Pollution

Digital persuasion environments enable misinformation to spread at scales and velocities impossible in pre-digital media landscapes because the structural incentives governing information flow prioritize engagement over accuracy. Research by Sinan Aral at MIT analyzing the diffusion of true versus false news stories on Twitter found that false information reached 1,500 people 6 times faster than accurate information, with false political news showing the most dramatic propagation advantage. The mechanism driving this differential lies in the emotional profile of misinformation: fabricated stories are engineered to maximize emotional arousal through novelty, surprise, and outrage—precisely the qualities that trigger sharing behavior. Accurate information, constrained by correspondence to reality, typically proves less emotionally provocative. Someone encountering accurate information about incremental policy changes experiences moderate interest; someone encountering false information about politicians operating child trafficking rings experiences intense outrage that demands sharing to warn others. Platform algorithms reward content that generates intense engagement regardless of its veracity, creating a systematic advantage for misinformation in the attention economy.

The persuasive impact of misinformation extends beyond individual false claims to broader epistemic pollution that undermines audiences' capacity to distinguish true from false information generally. When researchers studying misinformation effects expose experimental subjects to mixtures of accurate and fabricated news stories, they find that misinformation exposure produces not just acceptance of specific false claims but rather generalized uncertainty that erodes confidence in factual claims overall. Participants who initially correctly identified accurate information as true subsequently express reduced confidence in those same facts after exposure to misinformation on related topics, even when they correctly identified the misinformation as false. The mechanism psychologists term "truth decay"— misinformation creates ambient uncertainty that makes all claims appear potentially suspect, benefiting persuaders who profit from confused audiences unable to distinguish reliable from unreliable sources. Political strategists exploit this dynamic through what communication researcher Whitney Phillips calls "flooding"—deliberately releasing massive volumes of contradictory information not to convince audiences of any particular falsehood but rather to create such informational chaos that exhausted citizens disengage from factual evaluation entirely.

Digital platforms' business models create perverse incentives that make misinformation more valuable than accurate information. Fabricated content costs substantially less to produce than journalism requiring investigation, verification, and expertise. A misinformation website can generate dozens of false stories daily with minimal staff, while legitimate news organizations invest substantial resources in investigating a single story. When both compete for attention in algorithmic feeds, the economics favor misinformation producers who can achieve competitive reach with a fraction of the investment. Researchers tracking misinformation economics documented numerous instances in which fabricated content websites generate higher advertising revenue than legitimate news sources covering the same topics, because false stories optimize for engagement metrics that determine advertising rates. A fabricated story headlined "Governor Announces Mandatory Gun Confiscation Starting Next Month" generates vastly more engagement than accurate reporting on actual gun legislation, translating into higher advertising income despite being completely false. This economic reality means that misinformation represents not merely accidental errors but rather systematic production responding to platform incentive structures that reward engagement over accuracy.

The collaborative filtering algorithms that determine content visibility create additional vulnerabilities to misinformation through what computer scientists term "algorithmic amplification bubbles." When platforms identify that certain users consistently engage with misinformation, algorithms categorize them as audiences receptive to similar content, then systematically expose them to additional misinformation while suppressing corrections or fact-checks that algorithms predict will generate low engagement. Research by Facebook's own data scientists, revealed through internal documents obtained by whistleblower Frances Haugen, demonstrated that the platform's algorithms identified that users engaging with COVID-19 misinformation showed substantially higher engagement rates than users consuming accurate health information. Rather than addressing this by promoting authoritative health information, the algorithms optimized for engagement by showing users more of whichever content type—accurate or false—generated stronger engagement signals. Users consuming misinformation received algorithmically boosted exposure to additional misinformation, while fact-checks and corrections were systematically suppressed because they generated lower engagement metrics. The platform essentially created separate information ecosystems in which misinformation circulated freely among receptive audiences, while accurate information struggled to penetrate these algorithmic bubbles.

Digital Literacy and Resistance Strategies

Developing effective resistance to digital persuasion requires cultivating meta-cognitive awareness of the structural features that make online environments manipulative rather than focusing exclusively on evaluating individual message content. Traditional media literacy emphasized analyzing source credibility, identifying logical fallacies, and detecting emotional manipulation in specific messages—skills that remain valuable but are insufficient in digital contexts, where algorithmic curation determines which messages individuals encounter. Digital literacy demands understanding the business models underlying platforms, recognizing how interface design features promote particular behaviors, identifying when recommendation algorithms are funneling attention toward specific content types, and developing conscious practices that resist platform defaults. Someone scrolling through Instagram needs not just the ability to evaluate individual post credibility but rather awareness that the sequence of posts they're viewing has been algorithmically selected to maximize their continued scrolling, with content chosen based on predicted engagement rather than representativeness or importance.

Effective digital resistance strategies involve creating intentional friction that disrupts the seamless persuasion flows that platforms engineer. Browser extensions that remove YouTube's recommended videos sidebar eliminate the algorithmic funneling toward increasingly extreme content. Applications that hide social media engagement metrics reduce the feedback loops that reinforce performative extremism. Browser settings that block third-party tracking cookies limit the personalization, enabling hyper-targeted persuasion. These technical interventions prove essential because willpower alone proves insufficient against platforms employing teams of engineers optimizing interfaces to maximize engagement. The technology theorist Tristan Harris, former Google design ethicist, argues that digital persuasion operates through "designed addiction"—interface features deliberately structured to trigger psychological patterns evolved for entirely different purposes. The infinite scroll that eliminates natural stopping points, the variable reward schedules that pull-to-refresh create, the social validation that like counts provide—these features exploit vulnerabilities in human attention and motivation systems. Effective resistance requires not just strong preferences but technical countermeasures that restructure digital environments to reduce manipulative affordances.

Developing network hygiene practices that diversify information sources beyond algorithmic curation provides crucial protection against filter bubble radicalization. Psychologist Christopher Bail's research testing approaches to reducing political polarization found that simply exposing people to opposing viewpoints through forced-choice Twitter feeds often backfired, increasing polarization rather than lowering it. However, diverse exposure through what he terms "bridging organizations"—sources that present multiple perspectives without strong partisan identity—successfully reduced polarization by providing cognitive models for engaging complexity rather than choosing sides. The distinction suggests that adequate digital literacy involves not just consuming diverse content but cultivating specific consumption practices: following sources that regularly acknowledge uncertainty, seeking out expert analysis that identifies strengths in competing positions, preferring long-form content that develops nuanced arguments over viral posts optimized for emotional reaction, and actively searching for primary sources rather than relying exclusively on platform-curated information.

Perhaps most critically, digital literacy requires collective rather than purely individual resistance strategies because platform power operates at scales that individual users cannot effectively counteract through personal practice alone. Regulatory frameworks establishing transparency requirements for algorithmic curation, limiting micro-targeting capabilities, requiring explicit consent for behavioral tracking, and creating interoperability standards that reduce platform lock-in effects represent essential structural interventions. The European Union's Digital Services Act, implemented in 2023, mandates that platforms provide algorithmic transparency reports, enable users to opt out of recommendation systems, and face significant penalties for amplifying illegal content or for failing to remove misinformation during crises promptly. These regulatory approaches recognize that digital persuasion creates collective-action problems in which individually rational responses—accepting default privacy settings to reduce friction, engaging with attention-optimized content because it feels satisfying—generate collectively harmful outcomes. Effective resistance, therefore, demands not just teaching individuals to navigate manipulative environments but instead restructuring those environments to reduce manipulative affordances at the design level.

The evolution of digital persuasion continues accelerating as artificial intelligence enables increasingly sophisticated targeting, message optimization, and behavioral prediction. Generative AI systems can now create individualized, persuasive content at unprecedented scale—thousands of unique messages, each calibrated to specific psychological profiles, each iterates based on recipient responses, each impossible to detect as machine-generated. The near future of digital persuasion involves AI chatbots conducting extended dialogues that build rapport before introducing persuasive appeals, deepfake videos featuring trusted figures endorsing products or positions they never actually supported, and augmented reality experiences that seamlessly blend persuasive messages into the perceived environment. These emerging capabilities demand a corresponding evolution in literacy frameworks that help individuals maintain agency amid increasingly sophisticated influence technologies.

Digital persuasion represents not merely traditional influence adapted to new channels but rather a fundamental restructuring of how information reaches audiences, how attention is distributed across competing messages, and how individuals construct understanding of social reality. The persistent visibility of digital communications, the algorithmic curation that determines exposure, the quantified feedback mechanisms that reinforce particular behaviors, the economic incentives that favor engagement over accuracy—these structural features create persuasion environments qualitatively different from anything humans have encountered throughout evolutionary history or in most of recorded civilization. Navigating these environments effectively requires moving beyond individual-level skills toward collective responses that restructure digital spaces to serve human agency rather than platform engagement metrics. The future of persuasion will largely be determined by whether societies successfully implement governance frameworks that constrain the most manipulative digital affordances while preserving the genuine benefits these technologies provide for connection, information access, and democratic participation.

Chapter 10: Cultural Nuances in Persuasion Strategies

When Walmart entered the German market in 1997 with considerable fanfare and a two-billion-dollar investment, company executives anticipated replicating the phenomenal success they had achieved across the United States. They implemented their proven strategies: greeters stationed at store entrances offering enthusiastic welcomes, employees instructed to smile constantly at customers, baggers offering to carry purchases to vehicles, and morning cheer sessions where staff gathered for motivational group exercises. German customers found these practices deeply unsettling. The forced enthusiasm felt intrusive rather than welcoming; the insistence on bagging groceries seemed to question customer competence; the offers to carry purchases triggered suspicions about hidden charges. Within nine years, Walmart had hemorrhaged approximately $1 billion and withdrawn entirely from Germany, selling all 85 stores at substantial losses. The failure stemmed not from poor products, inadequate locations, or insufficient capital, but from a fundamental misreading of cultural persuasion dynamics that rendered their most effective American influence techniques counterproductive in a different cultural context.

This spectacular failure illustrates a reality that transcends retail strategy: persuasion techniques achieving remarkable effectiveness within one cultural framework frequently fail or backfire when transported across cultural boundaries. The mechanisms underlying influence—how individuals process authority claims, respond to emotional appeals, interpret personal relationships in business contexts, construct in-group and out-group boundaries, balance individual and collective interests, and assign meaning to nonverbal communication—vary systematically across cultures, fundamentally restructuring what constitutes effective persuasion. A negotiation strategy considered assertive and confidence-inspiring in New York may register as aggressive and relationship-destroying in Tokyo. An advertisement emphasizing individual achievement and standing out from peers resonates powerfully in Melbourne but alienates audiences in Seoul, where group harmony supersedes personal distinction. A sales approach built on developing extensive personal relationships before business discussions seems inefficient and manipulative in Munich but represents the only legitimate path to commercial trust in Riyadh. These differences reflect not superficial stylistic preferences but deeply rooted cultural values, historical experiences, linguistic structures, and social organization patterns that shape the fundamental architecture of persuasion in each context.

High-Context Versus Low-Context Communication Cultures

Anthropologist Edward Hall's distinction between high-context and low-context communication cultures provides an essential framework for understanding cross-cultural persuasion dynamics. In low-context cultures—including Germany, Switzerland, Scandinavia, the Netherlands, and English-speaking countries like the United States, Canada, and Australia—persuasive communication relies predominantly on explicit verbal content. Messages contain detailed information, arguments proceed through a linear, logical progression, ambiguity is minimized through precise language, and meaning resides primarily in the words spoken rather than in surrounding circumstances. German business presentations exemplify this pattern: they typically include extensive technical specifications, detailed comparative data, explicit explanations of reasoning processes, and carefully qualified claims acknowledging limitations. Persuasive effectiveness in these contexts depends heavily on message precision, logical consistency, factual accuracy, and transparent argumentation. Someone attempting to persuade through indirect suggestion, contextual implication, or relationship-based appeals without explicit substantive justification would likely fail because audiences expect and reward directness.

High-context cultures—including Japan, China, Korea, much of Southeast Asia, Arab countries, and Southern European nations—fundamentally structure persuasion differently. Meaning emerges not primarily from explicit verbal content but from contextual factors, including relationship history, social hierarchies, situational circumstances, nonverbal communication, and shared cultural knowledge that need not be verbalized. A Japanese business negotiator might express disagreement through subtle changes in posture, slight pauses before responding, or discussing apparently unrelated topics rather than stating objections directly. Chinese persuaders invest extensive time establishing personal relationships (guanxi) before introducing business proposals because the relationship itself constitutes the persuasive foundation—the trust and mutual obligation created through shared experiences, reciprocal favors, and demonstrated reliability matter more than specific proposal characteristics. Arab negotiations often involve extensive indirect discussion, establishing personal connections, showing hospitality, and building trust through tangential conversations before business topics emerge organically rather than through Western-style, structured agendas.

These communication pattern differences create profound challenges for cross-cultural persuaders, as the same message can be interpreted very differently across cultures.

Research by Jeanne Brett at Northwestern University studying international business negotiations found that American negotiators typically viewed their Japanese counterparts as evasive, indirect, and frustratingly unwilling to state positions clearly. In contrast, Japanese negotiators perceived Americans as inappropriately pushy, insensitive to relationship dynamics, and aggressively focused on immediate transactions at the expense of long-term partnership. Neither assessment reflected deliberate obfuscation or aggression; both resulted from fundamental mismatches between high-context and low-context communication norms. The Japanese negotiators were communicating clearly by their cultural standards—their nonverbal cues, contextual references, and indirect suggestions conveyed precise meanings to someone fluent in high-context interpretation. The American negotiators were likewise following their cultural persuasion norms, emphasizing explicit directness. The breakdown occurred because each group interpreted the other's communication through their own cultural framework, finding incomprehensible the very techniques that seemed most natural and effective to the other party.

Effective cross-cultural persuaders develop what intercultural communication researchers term "cultural code-switching capacity"—the ability to recognize which communication context they're operating within and adjust persuasive strategies accordingly. This requires not simply learning surface-level cultural customs but developing a genuine understanding of the underlying value systems that make particular persuasion approaches feel natural and compelling within each culture. In high-context cultures, this means investing substantially more time in relationship development before introducing substantive proposals, learning to interpret indirect communication signals, recognizing how hierarchy and social roles structure appropriate communication patterns, and understanding that silence, hesitation, and tangential discussion serve communicative functions rather than representing mere absence of content. In low-context cultures, it means providing explicit, detailed information even when it seems redundant, stating positions and objections directly rather than relying on implication, minimizing ritualistic social interaction that delays substantive discussion, and recognizing that what might seem like inappropriately aggressive directness actually signals respect through transparent communication.

Individualism-Collectivism Dimension and Persuasive Appeals

The individualism-collectivism cultural dimension profoundly influences which persuasive appeals resonate emotionally and seem legitimate rather than manipulative or misguided. Individualistic cultures—scoring highest in the United States, Australia, the United Kingdom, Canada, and the Netherlands—socialize members to prioritize personal goals, individual achievement, self-expression, and independence from group demands. Persuasion in these contexts succeeds by appealing to particular benefits, personal distinction, autonomy, and self-actualization. Marketing research analyzing thousands of advertisements across cultures reveals that American advertising overwhelmingly emphasizes messages like "Be yourself," "Stand out from the crowd," "Express your unique identity," and "Don't let others define who you are." These appeals trigger positive emotional responses because they align with deeply held cultural values about the primacy of individual identity and the nobility of distinguishing oneself from conformist masses.

Collectivistic cultures—including China, Korea, Japan, Indonesia, Guatemala, Ecuador, and many African nations—socialize members to prioritize group harmony, family obligations, organizational loyalty, and interdependence with others. Persuasion succeeds by emphasizing collective benefits, group approval, social harmony, and the fulfillment of obligations to essential others. Korean advertising research by Sang-Pil Han comparing Korean and American magazine advertisements found that 74% of Korean advertisements emphasized themes such as "We have a way of bringing people together," "The dream of prosperity for all of us," or "Sharing is beautiful." In comparison, sixty-nine percent of American advertisements stressed individual benefits and personal achievement. The persuasive power of collectivist appeals in these cultures stems from cultural value systems in which subordinating personal desires to group welfare is seen as virtuous rather than weak, and in which individual identity derives primarily from social roles and group memberships rather than unique personal characteristics.

These dimensional differences create persuasive pitfalls when appeals developed for one cultural context get deployed in another. International public health campaigns promoting condom use demonstrate these challenges clearly. Campaigns designed for Western individualistic audiences typically emphasize personal protection: "Take control of your health," "Protect yourself," "Don't risk your future." These messages assume that individuals have legitimate authority over their own bodies, that personal health concerns supersede social considerations, and that self-protection represents appropriate motivation. When similar campaigns were launched in collectivistic cultures using identical messaging, effectiveness proved minimal. Research by communication scholars studying HIV prevention campaigns in sub-Saharan Africa found that collectivist-framed messages emphasizing community responsibility ("Protect your family," "Don't bring shame to those who depend on you," "Your community needs you healthy") generated substantially higher behavior change because they aligned with cultural values prioritizing collective welfare. The same holds for environmental persuasion: campaigns emphasizing individual carbon footprints and personal responsibility resonate in individualistic cultures, while campaigns stressing community stewardship and intergenerational obligations prove more effective in collectivistic contexts.

Political persuasion likewise varies systematically across this dimension. Campaign messaging in individualistic democracies emphasizes candidate personal qualities, individual leadership capacity, and how specific policies benefit voters personally. American political advertisements extensively feature candidates speaking directly to the camera, personal biography narratives establishing individual character, and policy proposals framed as expanding individual choices or protecting personal freedoms. Political persuasion in collectivistic cultures operates differently: Japanese political campaigns emphasize party affiliation and group endorsements more than individual candidate characteristics; Chinese political messaging stresses social stability, collective prosperity, and harmonious development rather than individual rights or personal opportunities; Indonesian campaigns feature extensive family and community group participation, demonstrating collective support. These patterns reflect different cultural assumptions about legitimate political authority—whether it derives primarily from individual merit and personal leadership qualities or from group consensus, traditional hierarchies, and demonstrated commitment to collective welfare.

Power Distance and Authority-Based Persuasion

The power distance dimension—measuring the extent to which less powerful organizations and institutions accept and expect unequal power distribution—fundamentally shapes how authority functions as a persuasive warrant across cultures. High power distance cultures, including Malaysia, Slovakia, Guatemala, Panama, the Philippines, Russia, and Arab countries, socialize members to respect hierarchical authority, defer to superiors, and accept that power holders deserve special privileges and unquestioned influence. Persuasion from authority figures in these contexts carries automatic legitimacy; challenging superiors' positions or requesting explicit justification for decisions is seen as inappropriate or even transgressive by cultural members. Research by Dutch social psychologist Geert Hofstede examining workplace communication patterns found that in high power-distance cultures, employees expected clear directives from supervisors and felt uncomfortable when asked to participate in decision-making or to question management proposals.

Low power-distance cultures—Denmark, Israel, Austria, Sweden, New Zealand, and Finland — score lowest. Socialize members to question authority, expect justification for hierarchical decisions, and view power differences as pragmatic necessities that require continual legitimation rather than as natural social orders. Persuasion by authority figures in these contexts requires substantial justification beyond mere positional authority; subordinates expect to understand the reasoning, challenge conclusions they find unpersuasive, and participate actively in decision-making. Swedish organizational culture exemplifies these patterns: managers typically present proposals to staff for discussion and refinement rather than issuing directives; employees regularly express disagreement with supervisors without fearing retaliation; decisions emerge through consensus-building processes that give voice to multiple hierarchical levels. The cultural assumption holds that legitimate authority requires demonstrable expertise and persuasive justification rather than flowing automatically from organizational position.

These variations in power distance create cross-cultural persuasion challenges, particularly acute in organizational and educational contexts. When multinational corporations implement global management practices developed in low power-distance headquarters cultures, they frequently encounter resistance in high power-distance subsidiaries—not because local employees oppose the substantive policies, but because participatory implementation processes violate cultural norms about appropriate authority relations. A Scandinavian company implementing consensus-based decision-making processes in its Southeast Asian operations found local employees deeply uncomfortable with expectations to question managers, propose alternatives, and engage in open debate about strategic directions. The cultural disconnect stemmed from differing assumptions about legitimate communication across hierarchies: what Scandinavian culture coded as "respectful engagement" appeared to Southeast Asian employees as an inappropriate presumption blurring rightful authority boundaries.

Educational contexts reveal similar patterns. Western pedagogical approaches emphasizing critical thinking, questioning established knowledge, and challenging professorial interpretations align with low power distance values but create discomfort in high power distance educational cultures where teachers hold sage authority and student roles involve respectful knowledge absorption rather than critical engagement. Research by Jin Li comparing

Chinese and American educational values found that Chinese students and parents emphasized "learning as self-perfection through diligent absorption of established knowledge." In contrast, American participants stressed "learning as developing critical capacities to evaluate and question knowledge claims." These different conceptions produce radically different classroom persuasion dynamics: American professors persuade through encouraging debate and rewarding intellectual challenge. In contrast, Chinese professors persuade through demonstrating comprehensive mastery and modeling refined expertise worthy of emulation.

Monochronic Versus Polychronic Time Orientation

Cultural orientations toward time structure persuasive communication in ways Westerners often fail to recognize, because monochronic time assumptions permeate Western business culture so thoroughly that they seem natural rather than culturally specific. Monochronic cultures—particularly Northern European and North American societies—treat time as a linear, segmented, and tangible commodity. Schedules structure daily life precisely; punctuality demonstrates respect; meetings begin and end at specified times; discussions follow structured agendas moving through predetermined topics sequentially; multitasking is minimized in favor of focusing on single activities. Business anthropologist Edward Hall observed that in monochronic cultures, "time is money"—it can be spent, saved, wasted, invested, budgeted, and allocated. Persuasion in these contexts requires respecting temporal boundaries: making appointments well in advance, arriving precisely on time, presenting information efficiently without excessive tangential discussion, and concluding negotiations within culturally expected timeframes.

Polychronic cultures—including Latin American, Middle Eastern, African, and Southern European societies— conceptualize time as fluid, flexible, and relational rather than segmented and commodified. Schedules serve as general guidelines rather than rigid constraints; punctuality matters far less than demonstrating appropriate respect through interaction quality; meetings begin when relevant participants arrive and conclude when discussions reach natural completion rather than predetermined end times; multiple activities co-occur as people naturally multitask; relationship maintenance supersedes schedule adherence. Arab business culture exemplifies polychronic norms: meetings might begin substantially after scheduled times without apology because relationship-building conversations with earlier visitors appropriately took precedence over schedule adherence; discussions range widely across personal and professional topics rather than following structured agendas; negotiations extend across multiple lengthy meetings because rushing toward conclusions signals disrespect for relationship importance.

These differences in temporal orientation create substantial cross-cultural friction in persuasion because time-related behavior carries heavy meaning within each cultural framework. When American business representatives arrive precisely at scheduled meeting times in Latin American contexts and express frustration when kept waiting, their behavior—intended to demonstrate professionalism and respect—instead signals rigidity, a lack of relationship value, and cultural insensitivity. The expectation that business discussions proceed efficiently through structured agendas toward rapid conclusions feels appropriate in monochronic cultures but appears pushy and relationship-dismissive in polychronic contexts where extended conversation establishing personal connection constitutes an essential negotiation foundation. Research by business communication scholar Stella Ting-Toomey found that American negotiators in Middle Eastern contexts frequently damaged relationships by pressing for rapid decisions and interpreting polychronic time flexibility as manipulative delay tactics rather than as culturally normal relationship development processes.

Successful cross-cultural persuaders operating across monochronic and polychronic boundaries develop substantial temporal flexibility and reframe their success metrics. For monochronic-cultured persuaders entering polychronic contexts, this requires abandoning rigid schedules, investing significantly more time in relationship building before substantive business discussions, accepting that negotiations will extend across multiple meetings without clear predetermined timelines, and recognizing that what feels like a tangential personal conversation actually constitutes core relationship-development work essential for eventual business agreement. For polychronic-cultured persuaders in monochronic contexts, effectiveness requires punctuality, respect for scheduled meeting durations, prepared, structured presentations that progress efficiently through key points, and recognizing that task-focused signals professionalism rather than relationship dismissal. The deeper challenge involves recognizing that temporal patterns reflect fundamental cultural values—about whether relationships or transactions constitute primary focus, whether schedule adherence or flexibility demonstrates respect, and whether efficiency or relationship depth merits priority—rather than representing mere stylistic preferences subject to easy modification.

Face-Saving and Confrontation Avoidance Across Cultures

The concept of "face"—social standing, dignity, and public respect—operates across all cultures but carries dramatically different implications for persuasion strategies depending on how cultures balance face preservation against direct communication. East Asian cultures, particularly China, Japan, and Korea, maintain elaborate face-preservation norms in which causing someone to lose face through public criticism, direct contradiction, or forcing acknowledgment of errors constitutes a severe social transgression. Persuasion in these contexts requires extraordinary circumspection: criticisms must be delivered privately and indirectly; disagreements should be expressed through gentle suggestions rather than direct opposition; negotiations cannot force counterparties into positions that require admission of a mistake or acceptance of inferior status. Research by organizational psychologists studying Chinese business communication found that managers overwhelmingly avoided directly rejecting subordinates' proposals, even when substantial problems existed; instead, they would ask probing questions to highlight issues, suggest additional analysis, or allow problematic proposals to quietly die through inaction rather than explicitly reject them, which would cause face loss.

Western cultures, particularly Northern European and North American societies, maintain comparatively weaker face-preservation norms. While personal dignity matters, cultural values emphasizing direct communication, transparent disagreement, and separating personal worth from positional correctness create environments in which contradiction, criticism, and explicit disagreement carry less face threat. American business culture exemplifies this pattern:

colleagues regularly disagree openly in meetings, critical feedback is delivered directly in performance reviews, proposals are rejected with explicit explanations of deficiencies, and constructive conflict is often valued for generating better decisions through the clash of ideas. The cultural assumption holds that robust exchange of competing views serves collective interests and that personal worth remains separate from whether specific positions prevail in discussions.

These divergent face-preservation norms create predictable cross-cultural persuasion problems. When Western persuaders employ their culturally typical direct disagreement approaches in East Asian contexts, they inadvertently cause severe face loss that poisons relationships and undermines persuasive objectives. A Dutch executive explicitly pointing out Japanese counterpart errors during negotiations—behavior seeming appropriately direct and problem-focused in Dutch culture—destroys the relationship foundation in the Japanese context by forcing public acknowledgment of mistakes. The Japanese party cannot explicitly acknowledge the errors without severe face loss, cannot directly reject the criticism without creating confrontation, and cannot continue negotiations productively after such face-threatening interaction. The optimal persuasive path in high face-preservation cultures involves private, indirect communication that preserves face: perhaps raising concerns privately through intermediaries, framing issues as environmental changes that require strategy revision rather than as past errors, or suggesting new alternatives without explicitly criticizing existing approaches.

Conversely, East Asian persuaders in Western contexts often struggle because their culturally appropriate indirect communication style gets misinterpreted. When Japanese negotiators express concerns through subtle hesitations, pregnant pauses, and gentle topic shifts rather than direct objections, American counterparts frequently miss the signals entirely, interpreting silence as agreement rather than disagreement too face-threatening to voice directly. Research by intercultural communication scholar William Gudykunst found that American-Japanese business negotiations frequently failed because both parties believed agreement had been reached when, in fact, Japanese participants had never explicitly consented, instead avoiding direct disagreement to preserve harmony. Effective cross-cultural persuasion requires recognizing these face-preservation differences and developing interpretation frameworks appropriate to each cultural context—learning to hear disagreement in silence and hesitation in high-context cultures, while developing thicker skin to direct criticism in low-context Western environments.

The persuasive implications extend beyond individual negotiations to broader marketing and public communication strategies. Consumer complaint handling exemplifies these cultural differences dramatically: Western companies typically handle complaints by acknowledging the problem, offering explicit apologies, and providing concrete remediation. East Asian companies approach complaints as face-threatening events requiring elaborate, indirect responses: initial responses might acknowledge customer inconvenience without admitting company error, solutions are framed as goodwill gestures rather than admissions of fault, and resolution processes preserve both company and customer face through carefully choreographed exchanges. Neither approach translates effectively across cultural boundaries—Western directness seems callous and legally risky in East Asian markets, while East Asian indirection frustrates Western customers expecting clear accountability.

Linguistic Structure and Persuasive Reasoning Patterns

Language structure itself shapes persuasive reasoning patterns in ways that extend far beyond simple translation challenges. Languages with grammatical gender systems— where nouns carry masculine or feminine classifications— shape how speakers conceptualize and describe those entities. Research by cognitive scientist Lera Boroditsky found that German speakers, for whom "bridge" (die Brücke) is grammatically feminine, describe bridges with adjectives such as "elegant," "fragile," and "slender." In contrast, Spanish speakers, for whom "bridge" (el puente) is grammatically masculine, employ descriptors like "strong," "sturdy," and "towering." These linguistic patterns influence persuasive communication by channeling metaphors, analogies, and descriptive frameworks along gender-congruent paths that feel natural to native speakers but may not translate effectively across languages.

More profoundly, languages differ in whether they grammatically mark evidentiality—the source and certainty of information. Turkish, Quechua, and many indigenous American languages require speakers to grammatically indicate whether information comes from direct observation, inference, hearsay, or general knowledge through obligatory verbal suffixes. In Turkish, speakers cannot simply assert "She went to the store" without grammatically specifying whether they witnessed the departure, heard about it from others, or inferred it from evidence. This grammatical requirement trains Turkish speakers to habitually track information sources and assess claim reliability—cognitive habits directly relevant to persuasion. English lacks grammatical evidentiality, allowing speakers to make claims without specifying an evidential basis. This linguistic difference may partially explain research findings by cognitive anthropologist Asifa Majid showing that Turkish speakers consistently outperform English speakers on tasks requiring tracking information sources and assessing claim reliability.

These linguistic variations influence persuasive argumentation patterns across cultures. Japanese argumentation typically follows the kishōtenketsu structure: introduction establishing context (ki), development elaborating the situation (shō), twist introducing a seemingly unrelated perspective (ten), and conclusion reconciling elements (ketsu). This pattern contrasts sharply with Western logical argumentation, which follows thesis-antithesis-synthesis or claim-evidence-warrant structures. Persuasive writing that seems poorly organized and tangential to Western readers might follow impeccable kishōtenketsu logic, clear to Japanese audiences. Arab rhetorical traditions emphasize musayara (decorative elaboration) and takrar (repetition with variation) as markers of persuasive excellence—techniques Western audiences might interpret as verbose redundancy. Still, Arab audiences recognize that it demonstrates rhetorical mastery and respect for the audience through beautiful language. Adapting persuasion across these linguistic-rhetorical boundaries requires not merely translating words but restructuring entire argumentative frameworks to align with the target culture's reasoning patterns.

Understanding cultural nuances in persuasion ultimately demands recognizing that influence techniques reflect deep cultural values, historical experiences, and meaning-making systems rather than universal psychological mechanisms requiring only superficial adaptation. The most effective cross-cultural persuaders develop genuine cultural competence through extended immersion, language acquisition, and relationship-building within target cultures rather than applying formulaic adjustment checklists to strategies designed for their home cultural contexts. They recognize that persuasion works precisely because it aligns with how specific audiences construct meaning, evaluate claims, experience emotions, and navigate social relationships—processes fundamentally shaped by cultural contexts that cannot be reduced to simple variable adjustments but instead require thorough reconceptualization of persuasive communication itself.

Chapter 11: The Science of Timing: When to Persuade

On March 11, 2011, Japanese Prime Minister Naoto Kan faced an impossible decision. The Fukushima Daiichi nuclear power plant had suffered catastrophic damage from the earthquake and tsunami that struck hours earlier. Engineers presented him with increasingly dire assessments as reactor cooling systems failed. Radiation levels climbed. Explosions seemed imminent. Kan needed to order evacuations, mobilize emergency response teams, and coordinate with Tokyo Electric Power Company—decisions that would affect millions of lives and shape Japan's energy future for decades. Yet Kan made a critical error that crisis management researchers would later identify as a temporal persuasion failure: he attempted to gather comprehensive information and achieve consensus among stakeholders before acting, following the deliberative decision-making approach that had served him throughout his political career. By the time he issued evacuation orders thirty hours after the initial crisis began, the optimal window for protective action had closed. Residents in the most dangerous zones had already received potentially harmful radiation exposure that earlier evacuation would have prevented.

Kan's failure illustrates a fundamental reality about persuasion that previous chapters have not addressed: the effectiveness of any persuasive appeal depends not just on what you communicate or how you communicate it, but also on precisely when you speak it. Timing operates as an independent variable in persuasion success—the same message delivered to the same audience using identical techniques will succeed or fail based entirely on temporal factors ranging from time of day to position within decision sequences to phase of psychological readiness. This temporal dimension of persuasion has received far less attention than content and delivery mechanisms. Yet, research across domains — from medical treatment adherence to consumer purchasing to political mobilization — reveals that timing interventions often produces larger effect sizes than message optimization. Understanding when to persuade requires grappling with multiple temporal frameworks simultaneously: biological rhythms that govern cognitive function throughout daily cycles, psychological readiness stages that determine receptivity to different message types, decision journey positions that create windows of maximum influence, and life transition moments that temporarily increase persuadability across domains.

Chronopsychology and the Architecture of Daily Persuasion Windows

Human cognitive capabilities fluctuate systematically across twenty-four-hour cycles following circadian rhythms that evolution optimized for survival in environments where daylight determined activity periods. These biological oscillations create predictable variations in the mental resources available for processing persuasive appeals, with profound implications for when persuaders should deliver different message types. Research by cognitive psychologist Mareike Wieth, analyzing over two thousand participants across multiple time-of-day experiments, discovered what she terms the "synchrony effect"—people demonstrate superior analytical reasoning during their circadian peaks (morning for most adults, late afternoon for evening chronotypes) but paradoxically show enhanced creative insight and openness to novel ideas during their off-peak hours when cognitive control mechanisms relax slightly. This pattern creates non-intuitive timing strategies: persuasive appeals that require careful logical evaluation succeed best when audiences are at cognitive peak, while persuasive appeals promoting innovative solutions or creative reframing achieve maximum impact during off-peak periods, when reduced cognitive inhibition allows unconventional connections.

The daily fluctuations in what psychologists call "ego depletion"—the diminishment of self-control resources through their use—create additional temporal windows of persuasion. Columbia University researchers examining thousands of judicial parole decisions across Israeli courts documented a striking pattern: judges granted parole to 65% of prisoners whose cases appeared early in morning sessions before breaks, but only 10% of prisoners whose cases appeared late in sessions just before lunch or at the end of the day. The judges presumably held identical judicial philosophies, reviewed similar case files, and intended to apply consistent standards throughout the day. Yet their decision patterns revealed that mental fatigue systematically shifted them toward the cognitively easier default decision of denial rather than the more complex evaluation required for case-specific parole approval. This depletion effect suggests that persuasive requests requiring willpower, complex evaluation, or deviation from standard procedures succeed at dramatically higher rates early in decision-makers' days before ego depletion accumulates, while simple, routine, or default-aligned requests face minimal timing disadvantages.

Neuroscientific research using functional magnetic resonance imaging to track brain activity across daily cycles reveals additional timing considerations related to reward processing and risk evaluation. Studies by neurobiologist Russell Foster examining circadian influences on decision neuroscience found that the ventral striatum—a brain region critical for reward valuation—shows peak activation approximately ten hours after waking for most adults, creating a mid-afternoon window where reward-framed persuasive appeals ("This choice will bring you benefits") generate stronger neural responses than identical appeals delivered during morning or evening periods. Conversely, the amygdala, which processes threat-related information, demonstrates heightened reactivity during late evening hours as cortisol levels decline and homeostatic pressure for sleep increases. This neurobiological pattern suggests that persuasive messages emphasizing potential gains and positive outcomes achieve maximum neural resonance during the afternoon hours, while fear appeals and loss-framed messages generate the strongest responses during the evening hours, when threat-processing circuitry operates with reduced prefrontal inhibition.

The temporal persuasion implications extend beyond individual decision moments to sequencing strategies across multiple days. Memory consolidation research by cognitive neuroscientist Jessica Payne demonstrates that information encountered before sleep undergoes enhanced integration with existing knowledge structures during subsequent sleep cycles, particularly emotional content that receives preferential consolidation processing. This finding suggests that persuasive messages aiming to shift fundamental attitudes or beliefs benefit from evening delivery timing, which positions them for overnight consolidation, while persuasive appeals seeking immediate behavioral compliance achieve higher conversion when delivered during peak cognitive periods, when decision-action coupling operates most efficiently. Pharmaceutical companies targeting physician prescription behavior have incorporated these insights by scheduling sales representative visits for mid-morning periods when doctors demonstrate optimal receptivity to complex product information but haven't yet accumulated decision fatigue from patient consultations, then following up with evening email communications featuring emotionally compelling patient outcome stories that benefit from sleep-dependent emotional consolidation.

The Decision Journey Topology: Mapping Influence Windows Across Extended Processes

Complex decisions rarely occur through single, discrete choice moments but instead unfold across extended temporal journeys involving multiple phases with dramatically different persuasion dynamics. Consumer behavior researchers studying major purchase decisions—homes, automobiles, education investments—identify what they term "decision journey topologies": characteristic sequences of psychological states that potential customers traverse as they move from initial problem recognition through information gathering, alternative evaluation, choice finalization, and post-decision validation. Each phase creates distinct temporal windows in which specific persuasive interventions achieve maximum effectiveness because they align with the psychological needs and information-processing modes characterizing that journey stage. Marketing that succeeds brilliantly during early awareness phases often fails during late evaluation phases, not because the messaging quality differs but because the temporal position within the decision journey determines what persuasive approaches the decision-maker finds relevant and compelling.

Research teams at the Ehrenberg-Bass Institute, analyzing thousands of consumer purchase journeys across multiple product categories, discovered that the earliest decision journey phase—termed "category entry" when consumers first recognize a need or problem—creates the single highest-leverage persuasion window in the entire process. During this brief period before consumers develop defined preferences or begin systematic information gathering, they demonstrate maximum openness to brand suggestions and minimum resistance to persuasive influence. Significantly, this window operates according to psychological readiness rather than calendar time; the category entry phase might last three days for someone who recognizes they need a new laptop before a business trip, or three months for someone who gradually acknowledges their aging vehicle will require replacement. Successful temporal persuasion requires monitoring for signals indicating category entry—someone mentions dissatisfaction with current solutions, researches product categories without a specific brand focus, or discusses aspirational states that require new purchases— then delivering persuasive interventions immediately rather than waiting for the prospect to initiate contact. Technology companies like HubSpot have built sophisticated "behavioral intent monitoring" systems that track website visitors' engagement patterns to identify category-entry signals, triggering immediate, personalized outreach designed to establish brand preference before systematic evaluation begins.

The subsequent information-gathering phase creates distinct temporal dynamics: premature attempts to close fail catastrophically, while patient education and persuasion build authority and trust. During this journey stage, consumers seek comprehensive information, compare alternatives systematically, and resent persuasive pressure that attempts to truncate their evaluation process. Research by marketing scholar Jonah Berger tracking consumer decision journeys found that sales approaches emphasizing immediate action during information-gathering phases reduced the likelihood of purchase by 37% compared to methods that provided extensive educational content without purchase pressure. The optimal temporal persuasion strategy during this phase involves positioning as a helpful information resource rather than an eager seller, providing comparative data that transparently acknowledges competitors' strengths alongside your offerings' advantages, and demonstrating patience that signals confidence in your solution's merit. The persuasive payoff arrives later, when consumers complete their information gathering and transition into the choice-finalization phases, where relationships established through patient education convert to preference at rates substantially higher than those for prospects encountering brands only during late-stage evaluation.

The transition between decision journey phases creates particularly potent persuasion windows because these liminal moments involve heightened uncertainty and receptivity to guidance. When consumers exhaust productive information-gathering without achieving clarity about optimal choices, they enter what decision researchers term "evaluation paralysis"—a psychological state characterized by information overload, difficulty comparing complex alternatives, and a desire for simplification. This temporal window creates an opportunity for persuasive interventions that reduce complexity through clear frameworks, authoritative recommendations, or social proof demonstrating consensus. Consumer electronics retailers like Best Buy train sales staff to recognize evaluation paralysis signals—customers revisiting the same product displays repeatedly, expressing frustration about conflicting online reviews, or requesting increasingly minute specification comparisons—then intervene with confident guidance: "Given everything you've told me about your needs, here's what I'd recommend and why." The temporal precision matters critically; the same recommendation delivered during early information gathering feels presumptuous and generates resistance, while delivery during evaluation paralysis provides welcome relief that converts to purchase at high rates.

Life Transitions and the Persuasibility Volatility Principle

Beyond daily cycles and decision journeys, longer-term temporal patterns create what psychologists studying behavioral change term "plastic periods"—life transition moments when established habits, preferences, and identities undergo temporary destabilization, generating windows of dramatically heightened persuadability across multiple domains simultaneously. Major life transitions—graduating from educational institutions, starting new jobs, relocating to different cities, getting married, having children, retiring—disrupt the contextual cues that usually trigger automatic behaviors. Someone who has purchased the same coffee brand for 15 years at their neighborhood grocery store faces a genuine choice when relocating to a new city where different brands occupy shelf space in unfamiliar stores. The automatic purchase behavior that made them effectively immune to competitive persuasion in their previous context disappears during the transition period, creating temporary openness to new preferences. Research by behavioral economist Wendy Wood examining habit formation and disruption found that people show three to four times greater receptivity to persuasive appeals promoting new behaviors during the six-month windows following major life transitions than during stable life periods.

The persuasive opportunity during life transitions extends beyond the specific domains directly affected by the transition itself through a phenomenon researchers term "plasticity spillover." When life changes force reconsideration of behaviors in one domain, psychological openness to change generalizes somewhat to other domains, even when no logical connection exists. Katherine Milkman's research on behavior change patterns following life transitions found that people who relocated to new cities were more likely to adopt new exercise routines, try different entertainment options, adjust sleep schedules, and modify dietary preferences—even though none of these behaviors required change due to the relocation itself. The transition apparently activated a broader psychological state of openness to novelty, making persuasive appeals in multiple domains temporarily more effective. Marketers studying these patterns identify specific life transitions that create maximum plasticity: having a first child generates sustained behavior change openness lasting approximately two years and affecting purchasing across categories from automobiles to insurance to entertainment subscriptions; starting new jobs creates six-to-nine-month windows of heightened receptivity to persuasion about professional development, networking behaviors, and career-related purchasing; relocating to new cities produces immediate high plasticity lasting three to four months followed by gradually diminishing openness as new routines solidify.

Sophisticated persuaders have developed systems to identify and target individuals during life transition windows. Financial services companies monitor public records for home purchases—which reliably signal either family formation or significant wealth accumulation—then immediately initiate marketing campaigns for mortgage refinancing, life insurance, college savings plans, and estate planning services. These campaigns succeed not because relocated individuals have a greater objective need for these products than stable residents do, but because the timing capitalizes on temporary increases in persuasibility during transition periods. Similarly, companies like Amazon track purchasing pattern shifts that signal life transitions: someone buying baby products for the first time receives immediate targeted marketing for parenting books, nursery furniture, and child care services; someone purchasing business attire after years of casual clothing purchases receives professional development course recommendations and career coaching offers. The temporal precision of these interventions—delivering persuasive messages within days of transition signals rather than months later after new routines stabilize—determines their effectiveness.

Seasonal Patterns and the Annual Persuasion Cycle

Human behavior demonstrates robust seasonal variations driven by complex interactions among environmental factors, cultural rhythms, and psychological patterns that create annual cycles of varying persuasion receptivity. The "fresh start effect" documented by behavioral scientists Katherine Milkman, Jason Riis, and Hengchen Dai reveals that temporal landmarks separating old from new time periods—particularly New Year's Day but also birthdays, month beginnings, and Monday mornings—trigger increased motivation for behavioral change. It heightened receptivity to persuasive appeals promoting self-improvement. Analysis of Google search patterns shows that searches for terms like "diet," "gym," and "quit smoking" spike predictably during the first weeks of January, declining steadily through February and March. Gym membership sales demonstrate even more dramatic patterns: fitness centers generate 40% of annual new membership revenue in January alone, capitalizing on fresh-start motivation that temporarily overcomes the same reluctance to commit that kept people from buying memberships in preceding months.

The fresh start effect operates through psychological mechanisms involving temporal self-categorization and mental accounting. People perceive their pre-landmark selves as somewhat different from their post-landmark selves, creating psychological distance from past failures or suboptimal behaviors. Someone struggling with fitness on December 30th can reframe the struggle as belonging to "last year's me" on January 2nd, feeling that the temporal landmark provides an opportunity to implement changes without carrying forward past failure baggage. This psychological reset temporarily reduces the cognitive dissonance that usually leads people to resist persuasive appeals that conflict with their current behavior patterns. If I'm a "new me" in the "new year," then adopting new behaviors doesn't require admitting that my previous behaviors were failures, merely that they belonged to an earlier version of myself that the temporal landmark has rendered somewhat obsolete. Persuaders can either align with natural temporal landmarks by timing campaigns for maximum fresh start motivation, or create artificial temporal landmarks through mechanisms like "21-day challenges," "summer transformations," or "back-to-school fresh starts" that generate similar psychological reset effects during otherwise ordinary time periods.

Beyond fresh start effects, seasonal variation in daylight exposure, temperature, and cultural activity patterns creates additional annual persuasion cycles. Research by psychologist Saul Miller analyzing consumer spending data over multiple years found that people exhibit systematically higher risk tolerance and increased receptivity to indulgent purchase appeals during summer months, when extended daylight hours boost serotonin production and warm temperatures facilitate comfortable outdoor activity. Conversely, the late autumn and winter months foster greater receptivity to comfort-oriented persuasive appeals that emphasize security, warmth, and protection from harsh conditions. These seasonal patterns explain why luxury travel marketing emphasizing adventure and spontaneity succeeds best during spring and summer campaigns despite most luxury travel occurring during winter holiday periods—the summer marketing capitalizes on seasonal risk tolerance and aspirational thinking that generates initial purchase interest, even though the actual travel occurs months later during periods when comfort and escape from winter weather provide additional motivation.

Cultural calendar landmarks beyond fresh start moments create concentrated persuasion windows where specific message types achieve unusual effectiveness. The December holiday season generates distinctive consumer psychology characterized by gift-giving obligation, social comparison pressure, and temporary suspension of usual spending constraints, creating optimal conditions for persuasive appeals emphasizing generosity, thoughtfulness, and treating loved ones or oneself to indulgences ordinarily deemed excessive. Retailers generate 30% of annual revenue during November and December, not merely because gift-giving occasions concentrate during this period, but also because holiday cultural psychology temporarily reduces price sensitivity and increases receptivity to emotional rather than rational purchase justification. Someone who would carefully research specifications and compare prices before purchasing a two-hundred-dollar appliance during ordinary months might spend four hundred dollars on jewelry during December based primarily on how the gift will make the recipient feel, with minimal analytical evaluation. The temporal window creates this shift in decision-making psychology, making persuasive approaches that emphasize emotional resonance dramatically more effective than identical appeals delivered at other times of year.

The Refractory Period: When Persuasion Attempts Backfire

Perhaps the most overlooked temporal principle in persuasion is recognizing when not to persuade—identifying refractory periods when audiences actively resist influence attempts, regardless of message quality or delivery sophistication. The term "refractory period" originates in neuroscience, referring to intervals following neural firing during which neurons cannot be stimulated again, regardless of signal strength. Analogously, persuasive refractory periods occur after significant decisions, following intense persuasion exposure, or during psychological states characterized by reactance against external influence. During these windows, persuasive attempts not only fail but also actively undermine future persuasion by triggering defensive resistance, generating negative associations with the persuader, or prompting commitment to opposing positions through psychological reactance mechanisms.

The post-decision refractory period is the most clearly defined temporal window during which persuasion becomes counterproductive. After making significant decisions— particularly those involving substantial financial commitments, identity implications, or public declarations— people enter phases of decision consolidation in which they actively resist information suggesting that choices might have been superior. This phenomenon, termed "post-purchase dissonance reduction," involves selectively attending to information that confirms decision quality while avoiding or dismissing information that implies decision errors. Someone who just purchased a vehicle demonstrates minimal receptivity to competitive marketing during subsequent weeks; persuasive attempts suggesting they might have chosen suboptimal trigger defensive reactions that strengthen rather than weaken commitment to their purchase. Research by consumer psychologist Linda Price, tracking post-purchase consumer behavior, found that competitive marketing exposure during the eight weeks following major purchases generated negative brand attitudes and active recommendations against the competing brand to others, precisely the opposite of persuasive intent. The temporal principle: identify when prospects transition from the decision-making to the decision-consolidation phase, then suspend direct persuasive attempts in favor of maintaining relationship connection without challenging the recent decision.

Persuasion saturation creates additional refractory periods when audience members have received extensive persuasive messaging on particular topics, leading them to develop psychological antibodies against further influence attempts. Political campaign researchers observe this pattern late in election cycles: voters exposed to months of intensive campaign advertising demonstrate declining responsiveness to additional messages, with some research suggesting that advertising delivered during the final weeks before elections generates near-zero persuasive effect among already-saturated voters while consuming substantial campaign resources. The saturation refractory period operates through multiple mechanisms, including habituation (repeated exposure reduces attention and emotional response), counter-arguing sophistication (audiences develop practiced refutations for common persuasive approaches), and psychological reactance (perception of excessive persuasion attempts triggers resistance to maintain autonomy). An effective temporal persuasion strategy recognizes saturation risks. It employs pulsed rather than continuous messaging— concentrated persuasive campaigns separated by recovery periods, allowing psychological antibodies to decay before renewed influence attempts.

The principle of temporal persuasion windows ultimately requires persuaders to develop what might be termed "chrono persuasive intelligence"—the capacity to recognize and exploit optimal timing while avoiding refractory periods when persuasive attempts prove counterproductive. This intelligence involves monitoring audiences for signals indicating movement between decision journey phases, tracking behavioral patterns suggesting life transitions, aligning major persuasive campaigns with seasonal and fresh-start moments, and, most critically, developing patience to wait for optimal temporal windows rather than pursuing continuous persuasion regardless of timing factors. Research comparing persuasion campaign effectiveness across domains consistently shows that temporal optimization yields larger improvements in success rates than message optimization once baseline message quality reaches moderate levels. A mediocre message delivered during optimal temporal windows routinely outperforms a superior message delivered during refractory periods or at neutral timing. The science of when to persuade, long overshadowed by focus on what and how to persuade, emerges as potentially the highest-leverage domain for persuasion improvement in contexts where persuaders can control timing rather than responding reactively to unpredictable persuasive opportunities. Mastering temporal persuasion principles transforms influence from an always-on activity pursued continuously regardless of receptivity conditions into a strategically timed intervention deployed precisely when psychological, biological, and situational factors align to maximize persuasive impact while minimizing defensive resistance.

Chapter 12: Overcoming Resistance: Turning No into Yes

The human capacity for resistance represents one of nature's most sophisticated defense mechanisms. When Japanese negotiator Masaru Ibuka approached American electronics manufacturers in 1952 seeking licensing rights to the transistor for a small, unknown company called Tokyo Tsushin Kogyo—later renamed Sony—he encountered unanimous rejection. Industry giants dismissed the proposal with variations of the same message: transistor technology belonged in military applications and hearing aids, not consumer products; Japanese manufacturing meant inferior quality; and most fundamentally, why would an established American company enable a potential competitor? Ibuka faced resistance so comprehensive that rational analysis suggested abandoning the entire venture. Yet within eighteen months, he secured the licensing agreement that transformed consumer electronics. The turning point came not from overcoming resistance through superior argumentation but from fundamentally reframing what the resistance actually protected. Rather than positioning Sony as a competitor threatening American market share, Ibuka repositioned the proposal as an opportunity for American companies to monetize technology they themselves weren't pursuing in consumer markets while simultaneously establishing royalty streams from territories they didn't serve. The resistance remained—concerns about quality, market viability, and strategic wisdom—but its function transformed from barrier to bridge once the underlying protective impulse found satisfaction through alternative framing.

Understanding resistance as a functional response rather than mere obstinacy revolutionizes persuasion strategy.

Psychological research on resistance mechanisms reveals that "no" rarely means simple disagreement; instead, rejection typically protects something the resister values— identity, resources, relationships, autonomy, or existing commitments. Carol Tavris and Elliot Aronson's research on cognitive dissonance demonstrates that humans construct elaborate justifications defending initial positions not because they're irrational but because changing positions threatens self-concept coherence. When someone resists a proposal, they're often defending psychological investments already made—the public commitments announced to colleagues, the identity claims embedded in previous decisions, the relationships built on existing frameworks. Effective persuasion in resistance contexts, therefore, requires diagnostic precision: what exactly does this "no" protect? Only by identifying the protective function can persuaders design approaches that either demonstrate the protection is unnecessary or satisfy the protective need through alternative means.

The Anatomy of Resistance: Beyond Surface Opposition

The layered structure of resistance operates like geological strata—visible surface objections rest atop deeper concerns that, in turn, overlay fundamental psychological bedrock. When corporate executives resist operational changes, they frequently articulate surface objections about implementation costs, timeline feasibility, or resource requirements. These objections appear rational and substantive, prompting persuaders to marshal detailed rebuttals addressing each specific concern. Yet research by Harvard organizational psychologist Chris Argyris reveals that surface objections typically serve as proxies for more profound anxieties that feel too vulnerable to voice directly.

The executive concerned about losing departmental authority doesn't articulate "I fear this change diminishes my organizational relevance"; instead, they raise detailed procedural questions that feel professionally safer while accomplishing the same defensive function. The middle manager, worried about exposing skill gaps, doesn't admit inadequacy; instead, they question the training timeline's sufficiency or express concerns about team capacity.

This layered resistance structure means that addressing surface objections directly often paradoxically strengthens opposition rather than reducing it. When persuaders provide detailed responses to surface concerns, resisters generate new procedural objections because the underlying protective function remains unaddressed. The phenomenon resembles a game of whack-a-mole, where each objection answered spawns two more, creating frustration for both parties. Psychological research on "objection proliferation" demonstrates that when fundamental concerns remain unaddressed, the human mind is remarkably creative in generating seemingly rational reasons to support predetermined conclusions. One study tracking sales negotiations found that prospects who initially expressed price objections averaged 4.7 additional distinct objections after receiving price concessions, compared to 0.8 additional objections when salespeople addressed underlying value concerns before discussing price. The resistance itself wasn't eliminated by addressing surface content—it simply migrated to new justifications serving the same protective function.

Identifying bedrock resistance requires diagnostic questioning that excavates beneath articulated objections to uncover fundamental concerns. The technique involves what hostage negotiators term "tactical empathy"—a demonstration of understanding so profound that resisters feel safe revealing their authentic concerns rather than maintaining a defensive posture. Rather than immediately rebutting stated objections, effective persuaders employ what psychologist Arthur Aron calls "graduated vulnerability exchange," where the persuader first demonstrates their own uncertainty or acknowledges legitimate complexity, creating psychological safety for resisters to move beyond rehearsed deflections. A technology consultant encountering resistance might respond: "The implementation timeline you've questioned makes sense as a concern. What I'm genuinely uncertain about is whether the timeline represents your primary anxiety or whether there are deeper concerns about how this change affects your team's core competencies or departmental positioning. I'd rather address real concerns than win arguments about peripheral issues." This approach signals that the interaction isn't adversarial combat but collaborative problem-solving, frequently prompting resisters to articulate authentic concerns: "Honestly, my team built their expertise on the legacy system. This transition potentially makes their specialized knowledge obsolete, and I worry about both their job security and my ability to retain top performers during the learning curve."

Once bedrock concerns surface, persuasion transforms from argument to architecture—designing approaches that simultaneously advance the persuader's objectives while satisfying the resister's protective needs. The consultant addressing team obsolescence concerns might restructure the proposal to position existing team members as implementation guides, whose legacy system expertise becomes temporarily more valuable rather than obsolete; include a budget for advanced training that enhances rather than replaces capabilities; and build transition timelines that allow expertise migration rather than abrupt displacement. The fundamental proposal—technology adoption—remains unchanged, but its architecture now addresses authentic resistance rather than merely rebutting surface objections.

This approach succeeds not through superior argumentation but through superior diagnosis and creative structuring that transcends false dichotomies between persuader and resister interests.

The Resistance Paradox: When Opposition Signals Opportunity

Counterintuitively, intense resistance frequently indicates higher persuasion potential than mild skepticism or polite disengagement. The investment required to sustain active opposition reveals that the resister perceives genuine stakes—they care enough to fight, suggesting the proposal touches something meaningful rather than merely irrelevant. Psychological research on attitude polarization demonstrates that people rarely invest significant energy opposing proposals they genuinely don't value; instead, strong resistance often indicates that the proposal threatens something essential or, paradoxically, offers something desired but frightening. A colleague who vehemently opposes a departmental reorganization proposal might actually perceive its potential value but fear personal inadequacy in the new structure; their resistance intensity signals high engagement with the stakes rather than indifference. Effective persuaders, therefore, learn to read resistance intensity as diagnostic information about psychological engagement levels rather than merely as obstacles to be eliminated.

This resistance paradox explains why master persuaders sometimes intentionally amplify initial resistance rather than immediately attempting to minimize it. The technique called "resistance amplification" involves the persuader temporarily advocating for the resister's position more strongly than the resister themselves, creating psychological space for the resister to moderate their own opposition. When a parent encounters a teenager's resistance to college applications, resistance amplification might sound like: "You're absolutely right that college isn't necessary. Plenty of successful people never attended. Maybe we should completely abandon the idea—no applications at all this year. You could work full-time in retail or food service starting after graduation. That's a legitimate path." The exaggerated agreement paradoxically often prompts resisters to moderate their own position: "I didn't say I wouldn't go to college at all—I just don't want to rush the process or have you control every decision." The technique works because it removes the adversarial dynamic in which resisters feel compelled to defend increasingly extreme positions under persuader pressure. When the persuader stops pushing, resisters often naturally drift toward moderation.

Jiu-jitsu negotiation represents another approach, leveraging resistance energy rather than opposing it directly. The martial art of jiu-jitsu succeeds by redirecting opponents' force rather than matching strength against strength; similarly, persuasive jiu-jitsu transforms resistance energy into momentum toward the persuader's objectives. When customers resist premium pricing, conventional sales approaches involve justifying the higher cost through feature comparisons and value propositions—essentially fighting the resistance directly. Jiu-jitsu pricing approaches instead redirect the resistance: "You're absolutely right that our premium option costs more. Let me show you our basic package that fits your stated budget exactly." The resistance to premium pricing often then morphs into concern about missing premium features: "Wait, what exactly don't I get in the basic version?" The prospect's resistance energy now flows toward discovering premium value rather than defending budget constraints. The technique requires persuaders to abandon attachment to predetermined paths and instead remain flexibly responsive to the direction of resistance, constantly seeking ways to harness rather than oppose the psychological energy resisters generate.

The concept of "resistance debt" explains why rushed persuasion attempts that overcome resistance superficially often lead to delayed implementation failures. Just as technical debt in software development describes shortcuts that create future maintenance burdens, resistance debt describes opposition that appears resolved through persuader pressure but actually remains submerged, sabotaging implementation through passive non-compliance, delayed execution, or subtle undermining. Research on organizational change initiatives finds that projects with high reported resistance during planning phases achieve 73% successful implementation rates, while projects with minimal reported resistance succeed only 41% of the time. The explanation: visible resistance forces persuaders to address authentic concerns before implementation, while suppressed resistance manifests as implementation sabotage after formal decisions conclude. Effective persuaders, therefore, often deliberately create forums for resistance expression during planning, treating opposition as implementation information rather than obstacles to formal approval. The executive who encourages skeptics to voice every concern during proposal development receives implementation commitment after addressing authentic issues; the executive who steamrolls over resistance to achieve quick approval inherits resistance debt that compounds during execution.

Preemptive Capitulation: The Strategic Concession

The most sophisticated resistance-dissolution technique involves conceding elements of the resistor's position before they explicitly articulate opposition, creating collaborative rather than adversarial dynamics. Psychologist Robert Cialdini's research on "pre-suasion" demonstrates that conceding legitimate weaknesses in one's own position before resisters identify them dramatically increases overall credibility and reduces resistance intensity to core proposals. The technique operates through several mechanisms simultaneously: it signals honesty by acknowledging rather than concealing vulnerabilities, it demonstrates respect for the resister's intelligence by not expecting obviously flawed proposals to pass unchallenged, and it removes the psychological satisfaction resisters derive from identifying persuader weaknesses themselves.

Strategic concession requires distinguishing between core objectives and peripheral elements that can be sacrificed without compromising fundamental goals. A consultant proposing a comprehensive organizational transformation might preemptively concede: "This proposal recommends significant changes across six departments simultaneously. That's probably overly ambitious given your implementation capacity and change management resources. Let me suggest we eliminate three departments from the initial phase, even though I believe they'd benefit from inclusion, because I'd rather see three departments transform successfully than six struggle through inadequate support." The concession accomplishes multiple objectives: it demonstrates flexibility and reasonableness, it addresses legitimate implementation concerns before resisters raise them, and it refocuses discussion on which departments to include rather than whether to proceed at all. The consultant's core objective—organizational transformation—advances while peripheral elements about timing and scope adapt to resistance before it even crystallizes.

Calibrated concessions transform zero-sum dynamics, where every persuader's gain represents a resister's loss, into collaborative problem-solving, where both parties construct solutions neither initially envisioned. William Ury's research on "constructive conflict" reveals that successful negotiators facing resistance spend 68% of their time exploring interests and options, compared to only 32% on positions and proposals. The majority of the time investment occurs in what appears to be concessions and accommodations. Actually, it functions as diagnostic intelligence-gathering about which elements matter most to resisters and which represent negotiable preferences. A software vendor encountering price resistance might explore: "Help me understand your budget constraints. Is the total project cost the primary concern, or are they annual budget cycle limitations? If I restructured this as a subscription spanning three fiscal years rather than a capital purchase, would that address the constraint even if total cost remained identical?" The question treats resistance as information about the problem to be solved rather than as opposition to be defeated. Frequently, the diagnostic conversation reveals that surface objections mask deeper concerns—the client isn't actually price-sensitive but fears committing to long-term vendor relationships without escape options. The concession of "we'll include quarterly cancellation rights with full data portability" might resolve resistance that appeared to center on pricing but actually concerned flexibility.

The principle of "strategic vulnerability" extends the concept of preemptive concession into emotional territory, where persuaders admit authentic uncertainties and limitations rather than projecting false confidence. Research on medical communication demonstrates that oncologists who acknowledge uncertainty about optimal treatment approaches while explaining their reasoning elicit greater patient trust and treatment compliance than those who project absolute certainty. The admission "I've reviewed your case extensively, and honestly, the research doesn't provide definitive guidance about whether protocol A or protocol B will prove more effective for your specific cancer profile. Here's my reasoning for recommending protocol A, but I want you to understand this involves genuine clinical judgment rather than algorithmic certainty." paradoxically strengthens rather than weakens persuasive authority. The vulnerability signals respect for patient agency and intellectual honesty, both of which reduce resistance more effectively than false certainty that patients intuitively distrust. Strategic vulnerability requires courage because it contradicts conventional persuasion wisdom that advocates unwavering confidence, yet research consistently demonstrates that calibrated admission of limitations enhances credibility more than exaggerated capability claims.

The Resistance Lifecycle: Timing Intervention for Maximum Impact

Resistance evolves through predictable stages as proposals progress from introduction through implementation, requiring persuaders to adapt strategies matching the resistance phase rather than applying uniform approaches regardless of timing. Early-stage resistance typically manifests as reflexive opposition—automatic "no" responses protecting against change-related anxiety before the proposal receives serious evaluation. Psychological research on "status quo bias" demonstrates that initial resistance often reflects not reasoned opposition to specific proposals but generalized preference for existing arrangements over uncertain alternatives. Neuroscientific studies using fMRI reveal that novel proposals initially activate amygdala regions associated with threat response before prefrontal evaluation regions engage, suggesting resistance begins as an emotional reaction rather than a cognitive assessment.

Early-stage resistance requires persuasion approaches that reduce threat perception rather than advancing detailed argumentation. The technique called "normalization" introduces proposals as variations on existing arrangements rather than revolutionary departures, minimizing the threat signals that trigger reflexive resistance. A manager proposing remote work options encounters less initial resistance by framing the proposal as "extending our existing flexibility policies that already allow occasional remote work" rather than "transforming our work culture through location independence." The substance remains identical, but the framing activates different psychological reference points— extending established practices feels less threatening than abandoning them. Similarly, "incremental revelation" introduces proposals in stages, allowing cognitive processing to catch up with emotional responses. Rather than presenting comprehensive change proposals immediately, effective persuaders begin with conceptual frameworks: "I'd like to explore ideas about how we might better serve customer needs in rural territories where our physical presence is limited." This opening invites collaborative exploration without triggering defensive resistance to predetermined solutions. Only after establishing conceptual agreement does the persuader introduce specific implementations, such as remote service delivery models.

Mid-stage resistance shifts from reflexive opposition to substantive evaluation, in which resisters identify specific concerns about feasibility, resource requirements, or implementation challenges. This phase represents peak opportunity for productive resistance engagement because opposition has progressed beyond automatic defense while remaining open to modification before positions harden into identity commitments. Research on "confirmation bias development" reveals that resistance becomes progressively more entrenched as people invest time defending initial positions—early objections remain tentative hypotheses, but those repeatedly defended become incorporated into self-concept and identity. The executive who initially questioned a proposal's feasibility but then spent three meetings articulating detailed objections to colleagues has now made the resistance itself an identity claim; backing away from opposition threatens self-consistency beyond the proposal's merits.

Mid-stage resistance benefits from persuasion techniques that transform resisters from opponents into collaborative problem-solvers. The "co-creation" approach invites resisters to help design solutions that address their own objections, rather than having persuaders provide predetermined answers. A community organizer facing resistance to a neighborhood development proposal might respond: "You've identified legitimate concerns about parking capacity and traffic patterns. Rather than my team proposing solutions that might miss local knowledge, would you be willing to help us design parking and traffic management that addresses these issues while accomplishing development objectives?" The invitation transforms the dynamic from adversarial to collaborative. Resisters who help design solutions develop ownership of outcomes, reducing resistance through participation. Research on "procedural justice" demonstrates that people accept even unfavorable outcomes more readily when they participated meaningfully in decision processes. The resistor who helped design the parking solution agrees with the development proposal more readily than if persuaders had presented parking plans that addressed the stated concerns.

Late-stage resistance occurs after decisions are formally concluded but manifests as sabotage during implementation or passive noncompliance. This phase proves most challenging to address because resisters have typically exhausted official objection channels, leaving only covert opposition. Late-stage resistance requires different approaches than early- or mid-stage opposition—the time for modification and collaboration has passed, necessitating strategies that either neutralize sabotage capacity or create sufficient incentives for resisters to comply despite persistent disagreement. The technique of "small wins sequencing" breaks implementations into modest initial steps that demonstrate value before requiring comprehensive commitment. Rather than attempting a full-scale deployment that gives late-stage resisters maximum opportunity to sabotage, persuaders sequence implementation to build momentum through visible early successes. A technology deployment encountering late-stage resistance might begin with a single enthusiastic department, document measurable improvements, and then expand incrementally using early adopter testimonials to isolate holdouts. Late-stage resisters struggle to maintain opposition when colleagues report positive experiences and visible benefits accumulate.

Identity-Based Resistance: When Opposition Defines Self

The most intractable resistance occurs when opposition becomes definitional to the resister's identity rather than merely representing disagreement about specific proposals. Identity-based resistance transforms persuasion challenges from intellectual to existential, because accepting the persuader's position requires a psychological transformation beyond mere opinion change. When someone's professional identity centers on being "the person who maintains quality standards by resisting rushed timelines," agreeing to compressed schedules threatens self-concept coherence regardless of situational appropriateness. Research by social psychologist Dominic Abrams on "identity fusion" reveals that people experiencing strong identity-group alignment show measurably reduced processing of information challenging group positions—they literally perceive less thoroughly when evaluating evidence threatening identity-consistent beliefs.

Identity-based resistance requires persuasion approaches that provide "identity bridges"—frameworks allowing resisters to accept proposals while maintaining core self-concept elements. Rather than requiring resisters to abandon identity claims, effective persuaders reframe proposals as expressions of the resister's identity that are more authentic than the current opposition. An employee whose identity centers on "truth-telling iconoclast who questions management nonsense" might resist collaboration initiatives framed as corporate harmony-building but embrace identical initiatives framed as "radical transparency practices that eliminate political posturing." The substance remains unchanged, but the framing aligns with rather than threatens the resister's identity. The technique requires a deep understanding of how resisters define themselves and creative reframing that honors rather than dismisses those self-definitions.

The "identity elevation" technique transforms resistance by inviting resisters into more attractive identity categories that encompass the desired behavior. Rather than attacking the resister's current identity, persuaders offer pathways into aspirational identities the resister already desires. A physician who resists electronic health records because their identity centers on "an experienced clinician whose medical

judgment supersedes algorithmic protocols" faces an identity
threat from systems that emphasize standardization.
Identity elevation reframes EHR adoption: "The physicians
leading medical innovation recognize that advanced
analytics combining their clinical expertise with
comprehensive outcome data generate insights impossible
through clinical experience alone. They're not replacing
judgment with algorithms—they're enhancing human
expertise with computational tools that handle pattern
recognition at scales beyond individual capacity." The
reframe offers identity migration from "experienced
clinician" to "innovative leader combining traditional
expertise with advanced tools"—a lateral identity move that
feels like elevation rather than diminishment. The physician
can adopt EHR technology while maintaining and even
enhancing professional identity.

Sometimes identity-based resistance proves genuinely
irreconcilable—the resister's core self-concept fundamentally
contradicts the persuader's objectives such that no bridging
framework exists. In these situations, effective persuasion
acknowledges the impasse honestly rather than continuing
futile attempts at influence. The approach called "respectful
divergence" involves the persuader explicitly releasing the
resister from the expectation of agreement while
maintaining relationship integrity. A parent whose adult
child's life choices contradict the parent's values might
eventually conclude: "I understand that your path reflects
your authentic values even though it differs fundamentally
from what I'd hoped. I'm choosing to prioritize our
relationship over continued attempts to change your
direction. I won't pretend to agree with choices I don't
support, but I also won't make my love conditional on your
conforming to my vision." The statement doesn't resolve
disagreement but transforms the relationship from a
battlefield of persuasion into a respectful coexistence despite

fundamental differences. Paradoxically, releasing persuasion pressure sometimes creates space for resisters to reconsider positions they previously defended against constant influence attempts—the psychological freedom to change without appearing to capitulate sometimes enables the very shifts that direct persuasion couldn't achieve.

The wisdom to recognize when continued persuasion becomes counterproductive represents advanced influence mastery. Some resistance reflects fundamental values, identity, or circumstances that ethical and effective persuaders accept as irreconcilable rather than escalating influence attempts into coercion. The distinction between persistence and harassment depends on recognizing when "no" reflects conditional objections addressable through better proposals versus immutable boundaries requiring respect. Understanding this distinction transforms persuaders from influence maximizers into influence optimizers—achieving objectives where possible while respecting autonomy where necessary, recognizing that some resistance shouldn't be overcome because the resister's judgment and autonomy deserve respect beyond the persuader's desire for compliance. This recognition doesn't represent persuasion failure but rather persuasion maturity— the capacity to distinguish between resistance that requires creative problem-solving and that which requires respectful acceptance.

===
====

About The Author

Dr. Alex Mercer is a leading expert in psychology, communication, and behavioral economics, with over 15 years of experience researching and teaching the principles of persuasion. He holds a Ph.D. in Social Psychology from Stanford University, where he developed a keen interest in understanding how influence operates within societal and cultural contexts. Dr. Mercer's passion for teaching has led him to deliver engaging lectures at universities worldwide, and his work has been published in various academic journals and popular media outlets. He is the founder of the Influential Minds Initiative, a nonprofit organization dedicated to empowering individuals with the skills needed for ethical communication and influence in everyday life. Outside of academia, Dr. Mercer is known for his engaging workshops, where he equips professionals with practical tools for enhancing their persuasive abilities while promoting integrity and ethical practice. His approachable writing style and real-world examples make his work accessible to a broad audience, solidifying his reputation as a leading voice in persuasion.

About The Publisher

Welcome to The Book On Publishing

At The Book On Publishing, we believe in rewriting the rules of learning. Whether you're chasing your next big idea, building a better life, or simply curious about what should have been taught in school, you've come to the right place.

We're a platform built for dreamers, doers, and lifelong learners, offering bold, practical books and tools that empower you to take charge of your journey. From real-world skills to mindset mastery, we publish the book on what matters.

No fluff. No lectures. Just what you need to know, delivered with clarity, purpose, and a spark of curiosity.

Start exploring. Start growing. Start writing your story.

Read more at https://thebookon.ca.

Alex Mercer

Acknowledgment of AI Assistance

Portions of this book were developed with the support of AI. While every word has been carefully reviewed and refined by the author, AI served as a valuable tool for brainstorming, editing, and structuring ideas. Its assistance helped accelerate the creative process and clarify complex topics.

www.ingramcontent.com/pod-product-compliance
Lightning Source LLC
Chambersburg PA
CBHW062133020426
42335CB00013B/1198